Donated from

the collection of

Charles E. "Chuck" Kinney, Jr.

Lifelong professional horseman and

friend of Lake Erie College

A Horseman's Notes

A Horseman's Notes

Erik Herbermann

CORE PUBLISHING

First published in 2003 by
Core Publishing
PO Box 4771
Crofton, MD 21114-4771
USA

© Erik F. Herbermann 2003

All rights reserved. No part of this book may be reproduced, by any means, without written permission of the publisher, except by a reviewer quoting short extracts for the purpose of review or a distributor or retailer reproducing images for the purpose of marketing.

Disclaimer of Liability

The author and publisher shall have neither liability nor responsibility to any person or entity with respect to any loss or damage caused or alleged to be caused directly or indirectly by the information contained in this book.

ISBN 0 9723875 0 1

Library of Congress Catalog Card Number: 2002093645

Edited by Jane Lake
Page design by Paul Saunders

Colour Separation by Tenon & Polert Colour Scanning Ltd.
Printed in China by Midas Printing International Ltd.

10 9 8 7 6 5 4 3 2 1

In dedication to furthering equestrian ideals based on the nature of the horse.

Contents

Acknowledgments ix

Preface xiii

	The Illustrations	1
CHAPTER I	Overture to Horsemanship	7
CHAPTER II	Matters of Heart and Mind	11
CHAPTER III	The Physical Spectrum	21
CHAPTER IV	Communication: The Aids	39
CHAPTER V	Training Concepts	57
CHAPTER VI	Guidelines and Exercises	75
CHAPTER VII	Ever Learning	93
CHAPTER VIII	On Nature	105

Thoughts for 'On the Way' 109

Recommended Reading List 111

Cross-reference Conversion Chart 113

Index of Illustrations 114

Index 115

Acknowledgements

THE VAST CANVAS of horsemanship is truly a living, collective work compiled and refined over the centuries by many intelligent, dedicated horsemen. Riding would not be what it is today without our being able to stand on their shoulders. Their contribution of astute, detailed observations about the horse's nature continues to guide us unerringly to this very day. Illustrations of some of the masters whom I personally value most highly are included in this book, and their literary works are mentioned in the recommended reading list at the back.

Here I wish to acknowledge and express my thanks to those who have contributed to my equestrian education, and to my personal life.

On the equestrian front are: Walter Thiessen, Heidi Hannibal, Patricia Salt, FBHS, Monty Smith, and Dietrich von Hopffgarten. I am particularly deeply indebted to Egon von Neindorff from whom I have had the privilege of gleaning the practical foundation on which I have built my equestrian experiences. It has indeed been a unique education to have worked under the guidance of this equestrian artist – a master horseman if ever there was one. At the time of this writing, Neindorff has now faithfully served the horse and the world of Classical Riding for over half a century at his private institute in Karlsruhe.

It is with fond appreciation that I remember my dear friend Dan Aharoni; through his assistance *The Dressage Formula* was originally published. I also wish to honour Mr Joseph A. Allen 1910–2001. The horse world owes him much for his solid contribution. He played a masterful juggling act between the philanthropy of issuing works he thought had merit, and the practicality of keeping his publishing company running viably for 75 years. In an era in which the bottom line increasingly appears to be the criterion on which individuals base their decisions, he will be sadly missed.

On the personal front: I feel deeply grateful to have been assisted in my days by so many fine human beings, beginning with my beloved parents, Elizabeth and Joseph, and some extraordinary school teachers, Mr. Garnet A. (Tony) Parr, and Fr. John Hodgins – not to mention all that I have gained from the many fine people whom I have had the privilege of teaching over the years. The tolerant, kind acceptance of these dear souls who have endured my warts and peccadillos has been the patient soil in which I could do my quiet, inner growing. Thank you, friends.

A special thank you to Susan Dummit and John Pullen for contributing insightful feedback on the manuscript. The Buddha anecdote was brought to my attention by Jane Skiba. Permission to use the Anthony de Mello quote was granted by Scott Reeves.

My thanks for the authorization for the reproduction of illustrations given by the following:

- *Cheval gris pommelé,* oil painting by Théodore Géricault (1791–1824) – private collection – by permission of Bridgeman Art Library International, London, New York, Paris.

- *Tête de Cheval blanc,* oil painting by Théodore Géricault (1791–1824), by permission of Museé de Louvre, Paris.

- Sketches by Ludwig Koch are from his book *Die Reitkunst im Bilde,* 1928, Vienna (reissued by George Olms Verlag AG., Hildeshiem, Germany). Permission granted by Herr T. Brandner, Oesterreichischen Campangereitergesellschaft, Vienna, Austria. Generous assistance given by Frau Christiane Busch, Olms Verlag AG., and by Dr. Jaromir Oulehla.

- Photo of traverse, right; and the photo of piaffe on Andalusian stallion Juca, permission for reproduction granted by Egon von Neindorff.

- Permission for reproduction of Waldimar Seunig riding passage, granted by Frau Beatrix Zurek, representing the Seunig family. Kind assistance given by Frau Christiane Busch, Olms Verlag AG., and Karin Mueller-Stein Universität-Gesamthochschule Siegen.

– Photo of Johann Meixner in the levade, by permission of the Director of the Spanish Riding School, Dr. Jaromir Oulehla.

– The engraving of Pluvinel instructing the king from *Le Maneige Royal*, and the engraving from *School of Horsemanship*, François Robichon de la Guérinière, by permission of Mrs Caroline Burt, J. A. Allen, an imprint of Robert Hale Ltd.

– Illustration of Andalusian stallion Banbury Sampson, by permission of Sally Cleaver.

– The photos of Gitano and Pluto, by permission of Margot Huelke.

– Photo of blacksmith, Herr Glaser, taken by Dieter Schuchmann – private photo collection – by permission of Frau Erika Luy, and Herr Fritz Luy.

– The photographs of the author on Barty were taken by George A. Ross.

– The silhouette photography for the cover was taken by Thomas Bauer and Sigrid Sieber, with technical work by Hans Neukircher Neale, Foto Bauer, Karlsruhe-Neureut.

– The Hubble Space Telescope's edge-on image (STScI-PRC-23. August 2, 2001) of the ESO 510-G13 galaxy, revealing details of its unusual warped disk structure. Reproduced by permission of NASA and The Hubble Heritage Team: Space Telescope Science Institute (STScI), and The Association of Universities for Research in Astronomy, Inc., (AURA). Further acknowledgement to Christopher J. Conselice (U. Wisconsin, STScI). My thanks to Janet Hurst for her assistance with the images.

Finally, I wish to express my sincere appreciation to Mrs Caroline Burt for her invaluable assistance in guiding this project to completion; Jane Lake, editor; and Paul Saunders, designer, for having taken such care to help produce this book so beautifully.

Preface

THE MATERIAL GATHERED in this book has resulted from notes that I made during the decade of teaching since the second edition of *Dressage Formula* came out in 1989. In order to keep the *third* edition of *Dressage Formula* (published in 1999) within the scope of its original purpose – as a concise guideline of equestrian principles in note format – the bulk of the newly compiled and formulated material has consequently found its way into this current volume. In many instances, *A Horseman's Notes* fleshes out the terse skeletal structure of *Dressage Formula,* and is cross referenced to it, not only as an aid to finding related subject matter but also to avoid needless duplication. Nevertheless, occasionally some well-known, time-honoured equestrian guidelines have still been included, being among those fundamentals which I believe cannot be sufficiently repeated, heard, or read about, but above all, *lived*.

Because of the way in which the information has been compiled, *A Horseman's Notes* spontaneously responds to many of the common difficulties that might be encountered by any rider who strives to apply the classical standards in their daily practice. Those who work without instruction may therefore find it particularly useful. Though the text does deal with a broad spectrum of technical aspects, it accentuates especially the spirit in which we may best approach the horse and implement those technicalities. Furthermore, in the quest to define and express the ideals of horsemanship embodied in the exquisite light of the horse's truth, we are lead inescapably to realms beyond the purely equestrian.

This is so because the roots of this subject plummet deep, and cradle the principle components of our very being within the circle of its reality. Various metaphysical perspectives have thus been interwoven throughout the text.

The ideology presented is certainly not meant to be a litany of edicts pronounced from some lofty place of imagined perfection on my part. Rather, it is an expression of concepts and guidelines that I have found to be of solid value – the application of which continues to challenge me just as much as it would anyone else. Indeed, who among us is exempt from the deep personal struggle of finding harmony with natural law, the very pulse of the universe? Yet, is it not exactly through such effort that our riding and our lives grow rich with meaning?

Wolfgang Goethe observed, "Nature is the only book which offers profound content on each leaf". With this collection of notes it has been my intention to look anew at the endlessly diverse 'leaves of horsemanship'. Though ostensibly appearing ever the same, they are indeed ever new, especially when perceived through new eyes, new ears, and new feelings – new, that is, when enriched by yet another day of experience in the saddle.

May the thoughts expressed between these covers engender the desire to cultivate beautiful horsemanship.

Erik Herbermann
Gambrills, Maryland. March 2002

Note For the purpose of cross-referencing, each paragraph of *A Horseman's Notes* is identified with a number in the page margin. The first number refers to the chapter, the second to the specific paragraph. Cross referencing to the *third* edition of *Dressage Formula* appears in the footnotes. For those who own earlier editions of *Dressage Formula*, a conversion chart for the cross-reference numbers is provided at the back.

*Enter the sanctuary of the horse
ever with honour and respect*

Cheval gris pommelé. *Théodore Géricault (1791–1824). Canter pirouette left. Private collection. The Bridgeman Art Library International Ltd., London/New York/Paris.*

A HORSEMAN'S NOTES

The Illustrations

THE AIM IN CHOOSING illustrations for this book has been to present some of the finest examples of horsemanship which portray both technical and philosophical excellence in the classical tradition. Among the many wonderful examples are the engravings of Pluvinel's and de la Guérinière's work; Ludwig Koch's exquisite line drawings of work he observed at the Spanish Riding School; the vibrant paintings of Théodore Géricault; not to mention photographs of masters past and present – Johann Meixner, Ernst Lindenbauer, Waldimar Seunig, Richard Wätjen, and Egon von Neindorff.

In contrast to the considerable difficulty of finding instances of such perfection, it was certainly easy enough to find examples of not-so-perfect work – they were right there in my personal photo collection depicting some less memorable instances of my own riding. Some of these have been included as a study to see what effects the rider's crookedness, tensions, or other inappropriate attitudes may have on the horse.

Illustrations of the horse without a rider are also included. I believe that our observation of horses at liberty, as they demonstrate their phenomenal natural capacity while out at play, would have to be among the central pillars in our arsenal to help keep our perceptions and our work in the saddle on a viable, nature-oriented path as much as possible.

When first seeing Théodore Géricault's painting *Cheval gris pommelé,* see p.xvi, one may feel that it is just an artist's exaggerated impression. Yet, I am almost certain it is not, having witnessed one particular young Arab stallion who would occasionally do picture-perfect levades in his stall, with hocks barely inches off the ground, as the mares were lead past his stall on their way out to pasture in the morning. He would, in fact, hop around, doing a sort of turn on the haunches in the levade, apparently wanting to face the mares as they came and went by. Another remarkable instance was that of an Appaloosa gelding. When just turned out, he would not infrequently canter up a steep hill to a knoll at the top of his paddock, and perform two or three absolutely classical caprioles in succession. And, finally, I will never forget the vision of Hanoverian gelding Gold Tassel, formerly named Irrwisch, as a retired Grand Prix horse in his mid-twenties, entertaining himself by doing portions of advanced tests on his own while out at pasture. I have often regretted not having captured these incidents on camera.

With these experiences in mind, to me it is by no means far-fetched that a horse would do a canter pirouette with deeply bent haunches while at liberty. Yet, it is understandable that it may seem like nothing but fantasy to those who have not seen such things, or who have never seen others riding in such a way that the horse's hind legs turn into slow, elastic pistons, combining awesome power with deceptive ease, as the horse's mind, though eager, remains entirely calm.

One may similarly wish to dismiss the Ludwig Koch sketches as being merely a collection of idealized art. But we are fortunate indeed to have several excellent touchstones to help authenticate Koch's incisive observations. The one is a photograph of the stallion Banbury's Sampson at liberty p.56, demonstrating the beauty and harmony of balanced forwardness with a deeply engaged hindquarter, and perfect relative erection of his forehand; though full of energy, he is wonderfully calm and supple. These very 'uphill' qualities radiate unambiguously from Koch's depictions of the Spanish Riding School's work.

Before continuing, I must briefly digress to give heartfelt thanks to all those horsemen, past or present, who have remained true to their calling as custodians of the equestrian art, and who, because they have not sold their souls for financial gains or personal glory, have been able to leave

OPPOSITE *Ludwig Koch. Levade. The pinnacle of balance, and ultimate elastic compression of the horse's hindquarters. Compare with the photo on p.5.*

us with their illuminating and inspiring examples. For instance, we have the magnificent photograph of Oberberreiter Ernst Lindenbauer p.6 showing us that it is possible to achieve such independent 'uphill' beauty in the horse under saddle. We can readily compare this with identical attributes in the Koch sketch p.14. Similar correlations can be seen between Koch's depiction of the levade p.3 and the photograph of Oberberreiter Johann Meixner's levade (opposite). In all these works the artists have clearly created an admirably precise image of exactly what they saw.

The cover art is intended to portray unutterable harmony: a harmony which carries us beyond normal levels of perception, to find the ecstacy of connecting with the core of life itself, with horsemanship as the medium to that consummation.

In summarizing, much can be gained when the time is taken to absorb quietly and patiently the essence these illustrations radiate – to reignite an awareness and interest in those vitally important details of our equestrian science and art, so that these qualities will appear not only in photos and artworks from a bygone era, but may become a living truth once more in the daily practice of present-day riders.

Johann Meixner, Oberberreiter at the Spanish Riding School from 1885–1916. Levade. Indisputably, a Master at work. Notice the closeness of the hocks to the ground, and the softness of the horse's top line.

Ernst Lindenbauer, Oberberreiter at the Spanish Riding School. Working canter right. Perfection.

CHAPTER I

Overture to Horsemanship

WHAT COULD POSSIBLY be more sublime – intoxicating, really – than experiencing those exquisite moments of harmony with the horse, when we feel effortlessly buoyed-up on the full, elastic waves of his carrying back, and sense the awesome power, the delightful eagerness of this sensitive creature beneath us.

Here a little, there a little, serendipitously at first, glimpses of such fine experiences begin to occur to us, usually changing forever our view of what a true partnership with the horse could be like. In fact, the momentousness of those apparently small happenings seems to leave us with an irrational, bone-dry thirst for experiencing those extraordinary moments again. It is as though some irresistible force were compelling us inexorably to search for that elusive sanctuary of oneness – beckoning like the serene beauty of an emerald lake hidden somewhere deep within the mountains of our being.

In truth, the emerald lake represents a state of being whole, a merging with the deepest essence of the horse. When we are there, however briefly, we are it, and it is us. Likewise, when we are not there, that too, at that particular time, is us ...

On the other hand, the pathway to the emerald lake represents the process, the detailed, conscious journey toward that state. It is the living principle, the living law of the horse that we must come to know and follow with passionate certainty if we are to succeed in our pilgrimage. Not one false cell of our being will slip surreptitiously past the gatekeeper. In fact, the pathway is firmly barred to those who seek primarily for their own ends. Only when the horse is fully taken into account as a highly respected partner in the cause – his needs wholly and faithfully met – are the legitimate avenues opened, and can the metamorphosis of two-becoming-one begin to occur.

Reaching the emerald lake is an aspiration which taxes every aspect of our being: body, mind, and spirit. It is a journey which embodies consummate joy as it gives us the opportunity to develop and experience the potency and richness of our talents. And, with equal vigour, it confronts us with the exacting, prickly challenges of gaining control over our body, and to brave the less well-developed aspects of our spiritual being. Though it is at times a daunting and troublesome process, when it is taken on with clarity and enduring courage, it becomes immensely rewarding – especially as we begin to sense its far-reaching, benign undertones wafting like a gentle, healing fragrance into every corner of our lives.

All the qualities of a first class piaffe are present: the lowered croup, pure diagonal movement, ease and freedom of the forehand, and the weight-bearing front leg is correctly vertical, the horse is standing over enough ground. From School of Horsemanship, *François Robichon de la Guérinière, (1688–1751). J. A Allen.*

CHAPTER II

Matters of Heart and Mind

Introduction

*I*N THE QUEST TO IMPROVE our riding, the technicalities are often given the lion's share of attention when compared to the philosophical considerations. Of course, no one would deny the importance of technique, or that actions speak louder than words. Nor would anyone dispute that riding entails the joy of sitting on a horse, learning how to communicate with and guide him benevolently. But it must be equally clear that actions can be entirely unproductive, inappropriate or even destructive unless they are well directed by wisdom, intelligent consideration and wholesome attitudes. Surely, horsemanship is no more than a relatively crude undertaking in the absence of an evolved, integrated philosophy. In fact, we could view a sound ideology as the fertile soil in which the seeds of technique are able to sprout and take root, giving harmony between horse and rider the greatest opportunity to unfold.

The following points explore these matters in greater detail.

Setting the compass

2.1 Is it possible to create a work of beauty without the flame of passion fueling the endeavour? Surely, then, beauty and excellence in horsemanship must rest on a foundation of enduring love and respect for the horse. These mainstays of our equestrian art originate not from the intellect but, as with genuine friendship, they are an outpouring of benevolence from the heart.

2.2 Horses have the remarkable talent for reading our hearts – the innermost motives for our deeds. At times they even seem to respond more to our intentions than our actions. It is indeed stirring to see this in operation with horses who patiently take care of tiny children or awkward beginners. It gives insight into the value of having sincere goodwill toward our equine partner, and just how that alone can notably ease the task of learning to ride.

2.3 In matters regarding their nature, it is hardly surprising that horses can outwit the rider with considerable ease – after all, they only need to be themselves to succeed. This is so, because in horsemanship the task lies entirely with the rider to become horse-like, and not for the horse to become human. But, as we gain better understanding of the creatures and find greater harmony with them, we discover to our delight that they feel neither the need nor desire to outwit the rider, and usually come more than halfway to comply with any reasonable requests.

2.4 Riding could be compared to playing a game of chess with oneself, either winning or losing at one's own hand. But the marked difference between the two is that in riding the horses are on our side helping us make the right choices – if we avail ourselves of their counsel, that is.

2.5 In a uniquely tangible way, horsemanship challenges self-mastery in each element of our make-up: mastery over our spirit, the life energy, the very essence of our being which is directed by desire and motivated by will; mastery over our mind, which constructs ways of accomplishing our desires; and finally, mastery over our body, which gives us the opportunity to act out those desires and enables us to experience the consequences of our choices.

2.6 Through their astonishing sensitivity, horses show us that thoughts are things. Therefore, just as a correct physical position which is in harmony with the laws of physics is indispensable to allow essential energy patterns to flow through our own and the horse's body; so too, a sound mental position – constructive, wholesome, compassionate thinking which is aligned with the benign energy of cosmic law – enables *it* to flow through and strengthen all our endeavours. The horse innately respects and willingly follows such positive thought power. Conversely, our negative thinking easily disturbs the horse and results in distrust and fear. Without wanting to dwell unduly on such matters, I believe it is nevertheless worthwhile to review briefly some of the most common personal obstacles to success in horsemanship: immodest ambitions, arrogance, anger, irritability, having dictatorial or judgmental attitudes, impatience, lacking self-control (especially over our emotions), fear, anxiety, being inconsiderate, bearing grudges, resentment, or kindling vengeance in our hearts.

2.7 It takes strength of character and solid self-confidence to row against the stream of popular trends and to follow our heart towards things of deeper value, those rooted in the truths of natural principle instead. For if we are not constantly vigilant, any one of us can all too readily be driven by our unruly egos and selfish ambitions, or be seduced by peer pressure, or by financial, political and social considerations. The horse is seldom well served by these, and so often suffers needlessly because of them.

2.8 What is the difference between ambitions and ideals? Ideals are personal guidelines or aspirations we choose to set for ourselves by which we hold ourselves to a higher standard. Inevitably they encompass efforts at self-improvement, bringing us to direct our energies outward, away from ourselves, always ready to consider the welfare of others, whereby we become ever more useful, contributing members of the whole – better able to serve the horse, and to benefit those whom we meet, not only with our unique skills but with kindness, generosity and helpfulness. Through ambitions, on the other hand, I believe we tend to draw our energies inward to

serve mainly ourselves, satisfying our desire for self-aggrandizement, fame, power, control, or for the accumulation of material wealth – usually gained at the expense of our fellow man, the creatures, or the environment. Ideals, therefore, embody a desire for spiritual transcendence, inclusiveness and unification; whereas ambitions tend to be characterized by material expansion but at the cost of spiritual contraction, separation and fragmentation.

2.9 I believe that, when all is said and done, the only thing that will truly count will be what residue, beneficial or ruinous, our actions and efforts will have left on the souls of those around us, and on the creatures with whom we have dealt during our lives.

Who do we follow

2.10 In competition we find out if a judge likes our work, or if we are better than other riders. In the spirit of classical horsemanship, however, we seek to determine whether the horses approve of our interaction with them, and hold ourselves up to the light of their innocent and unassailable truths.

2.11 Taking this into account, we cannot help but conclude that the human judge's opinion could only be of value if it faithfully represents the horses' voice. Judging is therefore a mandate that bears exceptional responsibility, especially considering that the creatures are entirely at our mercy, and that their views are often expressed very subtly and in a language which requires considerable time and effort on our part to comprehend. Because of this the horses' 'messages' can so easily be dismissed by our intellect or overshadowed by unfitting or spurious desires. Thus, if we wish to grow ever more harmonious with them, it is imperative to be fastidious about working strictly within the horses' natural capacities – to guide without violating their joyful spirit, and to form the raw gold of

OPPOSITE *Ludwig Koch. A spirited, shortened working canter left. Compare with photo on page 6.*

their physical talents into a lovely jewel without damaging their health or warping their natural beauty.[1]

2.12 The clarity of vision needed to carry out such guardianship develops only after years of honest searching in the saddle, based on single-minded, incorruptible loyalty towards the horse. Through such impeccable intent and hard-won experience our sensitivity is awakened whereby the delicate rays of truth gradually dawn in our consciousness. In this way it becomes ever more clear how, through our benign interaction, the creatures become encircled in a state of wellbeing which unlocks the treasure of their astounding generosity to us, and how, through the struggle to adequately fulfill our equestrian task, we too are ennobled by having had to grow beyond ourselves.

2.13 It is up to us to initiate harmonious resolutions to any negative cycles which occur. The horses do not know how to do so, and tend to continue to resist (that which they perceive to be *our* resistance against them) until we help them out of their cul-de-sac by dissolving the resistance in ourselves first. In this way we give them nothing to be against in the first place (**4.49, 4.50, 5.31**).

2.14 For the true horseman the cultivation of willing participation is a sacred bond ... submission is equestrian bankruptcy. Willing participation is a joyful contribution based on understanding. Submission is based on coercion which usually leads to soulless obedience.

2.15 What kind of harmony(!) would ensue if we were to command our human partner, 'I *order* you to dance with me!' Is it really all that different if we wish to dance with the horses without respectfully inviting and encouraging their willing participation?

2.16 That which the ancients tell us is surely worthy of note: "... amongst those whom thou dost call thy friends and thine enemies, there is not one iota of difference".[2] With these words, are they not

---

[1] See the three-point guideline in the introduction to Chapter VI, on page 75.

trying to help us see that we can either validate and enrich, or undermine and make destructive, our relationships and experiences, depending almost entirely on how we approach the creatures, people or circumstances we meet?

2.17 What makes a tree strong but to endure frost, drought, heat, and storms? If we care to take up the challenge, horsemanship certainly affords us plenty of opportunity through which our character, our being, our soul can grow ever more resilient and sound.

2.18 Only through determined effort, applied over extended periods, are good habits formed and do unwanted traits gradually atrophy through disuse.

2.19 Riding is not a lottery. Through developing good habits we can paint the winning numbers on the equestrian lottery balls ourselves ... and at any time we wish.

2.20 How can we help but feel humbled when we see the actual measure of our being, relative to the staggering enormity of all existence, and realize that we only ever rediscover laws, truths, and principles by which the universe has already operated since the birth of time? In light of this, we surely experience nothing short of inexpressible relief and gratitude as we become aware of the mercy accorded us by universal law which abides patiently and surely, without our approval or understanding, and endures our misperceptions and foolishness as we struggle to find harmony with its unerring ways? Is it not exactly this simple, honest forbearance – the healing and forgiveness of nature – which is exemplified by the horses when they unfailingly go well the moment we ride well?

2.21 In the fullness of their unselfconscious glory, the dear horses help us find truth because they are pure, guileless reflections of it. Though language may fail our efforts to describe it, we sense truth as a gut feeling, a reflection we recognize consciously or intuitively as it reverberates on the soundboard of our soul.

2 The Teachings of Osiris. Also implied in Luke 6: 26–42.

2.22 What is an expert in any field, but one who has come to understand the natural laws on which the materials with which they work are based. The deeper the understanding of those laws and the closer one cooperates with them, the better the product. The fascinating thing is that the variety of end products is virtually infinite, while still remaining purely within natural law. So too the personalization of our riding, with the horse as our living canvas, is limitless. Our personality, our character, our general desires and emanations are all faithfully reflected in the horse. However, it is critical not to misconstrue the perfectly acceptable aspect of our individual stamp, which inevitably flavours our work, as being a green light for ignoring or violating the horses' fundamental make-up.[3]

2.23 Surely then, the power of observation of the laws of nature as they are expressed in the horse, and working in closest cooperation with them are essential qualities for the making of fine horsemen and women. It is the narrow path that must be followed by those who seek to become one with those intangible principles concealed within the tangible surrounding us. Yet, ironically, I believe that the degree of perfection achieved in this regard is not actually what matters most. That will be different for each individual depending on the degree of talent and a host of underlying factors. What does matter, however, is not only the effort we expend, and the heart with which we approach this subject but, above all, that we develop our understanding and skills in such a way that we cause minimal adverse effects on the creatures while our education is in process. Because, regardless of our level of ability, only when we hold the horses in the highest esteem and cherish their childlike enthusiasm, will our interaction with them be free of shame, and thus remain ever justifiably joyful and rewarding.

3 *Dressage Formula*, 3rd Ed, Chapter 8, 'Thoughts on the Nature of Art'.

OPPOSITE *Ludwig Koch. Collected walk. Note the clear, balanced 'oneness', and the head position of the horse which portrays the inner validity of the work.*

Egon von Neindorff. Traverse right, working trot. Beautiful harmony and dynamic 'straightness', based on the excellence of the rider's position and attitudes.

CHAPTER III

The Physical Spectrum

Monsieur de Pluvinel always sits in the same posture, up straight, whether he is putting the horse into the airs or at the walk; and I have often heard him say that for a Horseman to be graceful, he must never, when making a horse perform, move, except to raise very gently the arm up and down, back and forth, to make the switch whistle ...

MONSIEUR LE GRAND[1]

Introduction

THE RIDER'S PHYSICAL seat and position comprises not only the obvious external form, but also encompasses the full gamut of intangible attitudes which are inseparable from the mental position – the physical follows the spiritual. Thus, the body's outer appearance reliably mirrors the degree of understanding and development of our entire equestrian proficiency. The qualities of patience, modesty and kindness, for example, radiate from the physical as an ineffable serenity and gracefulness; and the simple economy of elegance exists only when significant levels of physical and spiritual harmony have been achieved within the rider themselves. These characteristics are implicitly unfalsifiable, and cannot help but spill over to reflect their likeness in the horse.

---

1 From *Le Maneige Royal*, Pluvinel. p 24. J.A. Allen & Co. Ltd. 1969. English translation by Hilda Nelson, 1989.

Though this chapter does unavoidably deal with technical and mechanical elements of body posture, numerous points describe attitudes, feelings or just 'ways of thinking' rather than necessarily implying the need for overt physical adjustments. Because of the inherent subtlety of such things, their intrinsic value only becomes more clear once relaxation and reasonably good control over the basic external position have been achieved. Finally, though for the sake of analysis the position attributes are discussed separately below, it is essential to keep the concept of harmonious orchestration of all our physical attitudes as one of our highest priorities, and to remain aware of the critical association between posture changes and their inevitable effects on the horse – it is the core principle on which refined aiding is built. Things work best when we always have a clear *external* purpose in mind (gait, school figure, exercise) as a backdrop for making any position adjustment.

A physical philosophy: where mind and body meet

3.1 Some riders may be peaceful souls but do not yet own their bodies; they are inclined to physical awkwardness because the wiring between mind and body is not yet well connected. Others might be physically well wired but do not yet own their souls, being as yet edgy, unpolished diamonds. Horsemanship helps us grow in balanced wholeness between mind, body and spirit.

3.2 The main inhibitors to the flow of suitable energy patterns through the rider's body are physical and mental tensions. Mental tensions may be eased through breathing exercises, meditation and visualization aimed at gaining serenity and building self-acceptance, self-confidence, patience and trust. Physically, it is essential to get the shoulders, hip joints, and thighs relaxed. *Movement* – doing longeing exercises (on or off the longe), or thinking of dancing (boogieing) with the horse while riding – is especially helpful to unlock our tense or stiff bodies (3.16).

3.3 An essential aspect of our leadership entails that we are able to 'think immanently'. This means we can think and plan ahead without these thoughts being carried into our bodies, that is, not until we are ready to tell the horse about our intentions. The value of and need for immanent thinking can be readily appreciated when we observe inexperienced riders who may run into all manner of difficulty only because, for example, they are unable to keep the thought 'canter' to themselves, or are unable to remain independent and serene when the horse gets nervous.

3.4 A purely intellectual approach to riding is not very effective. Things work best when we let our mind be constantly guided by living feedback from our physical senses and from our intuition.

The seat

3.5 Any time we think of the seat, the entire position needs to be taken into account. Equating the seat with the hips and seat bones only would be like having four wheels sitting in the garage, and imagining them to be a whole car.[2]

3.6 We must let ourselves *rest* straight down in the deepest part of the saddle, and end up '*resting* on the triangle', made up of the two seat bones and the crotch, *at all times*. It is the absolute foundation on which all competent riding is built.

3.7 To 'let yourself *rest*', is like a cat lazing on a branch. Rather than trying to 'make ourselves sit deep', we must literally be draped on the horse, letting gravity do the work. Then, without losing that *resting* feeling, think 'elegance'... carry a book on your head (3.37).

3.8 To withdraw any of the three points of the triangle from the saddle compromises the entire aiding system, because it causes the hand to become the dominant influence by default. When we rest on our

---

[2] *Dressage Formula*, 3rd Ed., 021, p 42, 'The driving weight aid'.

seat bones and pubic bone, feeling them in constant contact with the saddle, we literally become connected with the ground via the horse's body – because his body becomes our body, and his legs our legs.

3.9 To gain accurate control over the weight in our seat bones we must sit squarely in the middle of the saddle and in the centre of the horse with our shoulders directly above our hips. To achieve this I use an analogy of having two imaginary pillars located in the upper body, one on either side of the spine. Each pillar stands above its respective seat bone, and we must strive to keep them both the same. If one pillar is weak it causes the shoulder on that side to drop and the hip to collapse, which weakens the seat bone and the effectiveness of the leg and rein on that side. This in turn makes it difficult to maintain the horse's balance and straightness, resulting in poor control over directional guidance.

3.10 An effective little exercise to become aware of (or to correct) a collapsed pillar is to begin by getting the shoulders well back and down first, doing so by raising the ribcage and making a square upside-down 'U',[3] ending up with the shoulders and upper arm *hanging* well down through the elbow. Then *temporarily* actually 'lock' the shoulders there (obviously, only 'lock' during the brief time it takes to do this exercise). Then simultaneously stretch the ribcage away from the hip, and the hip away from the ribcage: first on the right side, then on the left, back-and-forth alternately several times, until a better feeling for squareness has developed.

3.11 If the horse is cutting *in*, besides being a sign that the horse is not adequately balanced, the rider is likely not sufficiently on the inside seat bone. To correct this, Pat Salt recommended raising the inside leg *a little*, which increases the weight on that seat bone and cures the cutting in. This independent raising of one leg, without leaning, collapsing or stiffening the upper body, can be used at any time to help get either seat bone better down on the saddle. Take note,

---

[3] *Dressage Formula*, 3rd Ed., 009, see 'Note' on page 19.

however, this is a temporary means to an end (getting a better mental connection with the feeling for having the seat bones more down), not an end in itself. We should be able to increase weight in either seat bone without having to raise a leg (see photo series on page 32). Generally, it is best to avoid turning corrective measures into methods.

3.12 Similarly, if the horse is cutting *out*, it is more than likely that the outside seat bone is not adequately on the saddle because its pillar is collapsed, or the rider is leaning *in*. Other reasons could be because the rider is pulling on the inside rein thereby overbending the neck, or the horse has not been brought sufficiently up to the outside aids, or there is a lack of outside rein or leg.

3.13 Though we may be collapsing only one pillar, the seat is actually totally defunct. Why? Because it is no more possible to control the horse's energy with only one seat bone on the saddle, than it would be to channel water with only one river bank. Having two sound seat bones on the saddle at all times, because of those two sound pillars, is the key to keeping the horse squarely under us, *laterally* controlled between the seat bones (the legs only become truly effective once that has occurred). By the same principle, the seat can also keep the horse under us *longitudinally* (maintaining back-to-front balance once balance has been established) without the use of the hand.

3.14 In essence, the energy pattern of each seat bone should be constantly over the knee on its own side. This can be achieved by thinking of kneeling (without pulling the lower leg back and up!), or dropping the legs off and continuing on down the road without them, or sitting beyond the knees (all these are subtle thoughts or essences).The horse will not reach properly into the bridle on the side where the seat bone energy has dropped behind the knee. Regardless of these points, always *let* yourself *rest* straight down in the deepest part of the saddle.

3.15 Should it be necessary to adjust the legs overtly, begin by taking them off the horse slightly, then opening the buttocks and the back of the legs and thighs, while having the heels outward, and toes inward, and then laying the whole leg relaxed on the horse – think of riding with the shins. This minimizes pinching with the thighs, and gives the horse's body, especially its back muscles, unrestricted freedom to move under the seat and between the rider's legs. Sit broad, and fat, and relaxed in the saddle. To help in the general relaxation of the seat, hip joints, thighs and legs, 'spread the toes wide, and be aware of *feeling* the sole of the boots'.[4]

3.16 Experimenting with the following concepts at the walk for a few minutes at the beginning of one's ride can help settle the seat bones on the saddle. This will be found especially useful if there is no opportunity to be properly longed. These are simultaneously signs that we are beginning to sit better, as well as being ways to achieve that better, more independent seat: **a)** whether we ride with or without stirrups the feeling in the seat should remain steady and deep and the same; **b)** when riding without stirrups we can either let our toes dangle down, or we can gently raise them (no more than 65 per cent to avoid tension) and deepen the heel (not jam it down) without the seat changing in its depth, steadiness or relaxation; **c)** we are able to lift (straight up, as opposed to taking the leg off the horse sideways, or lifting the lower leg back and up) and lower either leg, without causing tensions or changes in the position or squareness of the upper body/hips or the steadiness and depth of the seat bones on the saddle – both legs can also be raised simultaneously, but keep the lower back flat while doing so; this helps keep the seat bones pointing forward, and tones the stomach; **d)** because our hip joints, thighs, knees, and ankles are relaxed, our legs are able to hang relaxed and leaden, which causes us to feel as though we are hung on the horse purely by the seat bones and crotch, (again, while hanging the legs, keep the lower back flat and the seat bones well forward; see 'nape of neck' 3.20, 3.24, 3.25); **e)** we are able to turn the leg inward (3.15), and/or gently raise only the toe up (a slight, unobservable lightening up off the stirrup)

---

4 Concept in quotes contributed by Frau Ingrid Oehlert.

while *letting* the heels reach more for the ground without losing that relaxed, heavy feeling in the legs; f) whether we are doing rising or sitting trot, the seat feels the same and the horse feels the same, we do not lose the steady, unified, balanced, resting feeling. Scissoring with the legs, or doing the forward or backward 'bicycle pedaling' exercises with the legs are further useful adjuncts.

The position

3.17 An excellent position is like a beautiful, well-made instrument, ever prepared to be used for a delicate operation. It could be described as a 'zero' position because through it we carry ourselves independently, and totally harmoniously. It in no way either hinders or influences the horse unless deliberately called upon by the rider. A poor position is therefore like being 'in the red', because it generally impedes the horse's movement because of awkwardness, tension, or involuntary movement in the rider. Like trying to do brain surgery with a garden hoe, the poor seat and position cannot be used with the refinement needed to do excellent work. The logical sequence in which the seat and position influences come into play is described in **4.26**.

3.18 The last four per cent of the position corrections (that is, between 96 and 100 per cent) brings most of the good effects to our aiding influence on the horse. Anything below 96 per cent is mediocrity.

3.19 To maintain suppleness and sensitivity over extended periods, it is best to refresh the position instead of trying to hold it. This can be as simple as thinking of 'breathing in and breathing out' the position corrections; or we could 'fluff up our feathers' every once in a while, and pretend we have just begun. These concepts provide us with a new start that helps wash away the staleness from all our trying. By making a natural cycle in all we do, whether correcting ourselves or aiding the horse, we can avoid much unnecessary stiffness, tension and fatigue.

3.20 Let us review a few practical examples of how seat/position changes affect the horse: 'seat bones leading' (achieved through pelvic tilt [flat lower back], fill the nape of the neck)[5] means an increased driving influence, it keeps the horse in front of the seat. The general attitude of 'hips leading', 'tipping the chair'[6], 'riding the horse and hips through the elbows', means reach for and step through the bridle. 'Stretching' having a 'long front line', besides giving us a practical form, represents our positive commitment to forwardness. 'Broadening' (3.26) the front line (with a well-raised ribcage, which allows the shoulders to hang naturally back and down) is the basis for driving, or for 'sustaining' the contact when a horse resists; if these attitudes are used while 'stilling' the seat, and sustaining the contact, it means to halt or half-halt. These aspects are not actually isolated but need to be orchestrated harmoniously – not unlike cooking, 'a pinch of this, a dash of that'.[7] Also see **5.32** to **5.41**.

3.21 First position the hips (flat back, vertical pelvis with seat bones leading, pointing forward), then open the upper body like a flower.

3.22 The isometric contradiction of having the seat bones leading (without leaning back, and without taking the crotch off the saddle) while having a long, stretched, open front line (without hollowing the lower back) is that which consolidates our position into a useful form.

The front line[8]

3.23 Acquiring an open front line is based on a soft, liberating attitude, like gently swinging open a pair of large French doors overlooking a meadow.

---

5 *Dressage Formula*, 3rd Ed., 021.
6 See Müseler, *Riding Logic*.
7 *Dressage Formula*, 3rd Ed., 021, 022, 060; illustrations page 41.
8 *Dressage Formula*, 3rd Ed., 009; and see 'Note' on page 19.

3.24 An effective front line entails four distinct elements: **a)** raise the solar plexus (ribcage) *gently* up and back into the back of our collar, this involves filling the nape of the neck (**3.25**); **b)** shoulders hanging naturally back and down, relaxed through the elbows (end up showing the front of the arm pits); **c)** bent, pointy, *heavy*, relaxed elbows; **d)** vertical hands. These combined make up the core position attitude which allows the circuit to be completed.[9]

3.25 To elaborate on point **a)** above, just like the horse, we too must 'raise' our withers[10] (imagine being on all fours). This is done by a combination of raising the solar plexus (ribcage) up and back into the back of our collar, and filling the nape of the neck (gently pressing it) into the back of the collar as well. We must keep our ears far from our shoulders; the shoulders far from the ears at all times: 'chin in, ears up',[11] (but avoid getting a double chin by forcing the 'chin in' concept). The importance of filling the nape of the neck cannot be overstated, since this correctly stretches our spine, and gives our lower back (the lumbar vertebrae) the necessary substance to be effective, and also less likelihood of being hollowed. To elaborate on point **b)**: if the shoulders are very rounded or stiff, then doing several square upside-down 'U's [see footnote[8]] in succession each day will help get the muscles and connective tissue stretched sufficiently that just doing the recommendations of point **a)** will cause the shoulders to end up hanging more naturally down through the spine when looking at the rider from the side. These points serve to avoid the mistake of trying to 'hold' the correct shoulder position which only causes unwanted tensions.

3.26 Once a correct, 'zero' position has been achieved through 'opening' the front line, we can then use it (it becomes an actual aid) by

---

9 *Dressage Formula*, 3rd Ed., 041, and 009.

10 Just like the horse's withers, though considerably less prominent, our withers is located between and just above the shoulder blades. It is made up of the upper thoracic vertebrae, and form the base on which the cervical vertebrae rest.

11 Concept in quotes, Paul Turner.

'broadening'[12] it, particularly at the stomach, navel and solar plexus, and down into the pelvic region. This would be emphasized during moments of driving, transitions, and halting or half-halting, or when temporarily needing to 'sustain' the contact when the horse is against the bit, for example. Such broadening should be used in conjunction with suitable driving attitudes, i.e. 'tipping the chair',[13] and riding the hips through the elbows.

3.27 The *bent* elbow is an essential conversion point for the energy. Collectively, the four points mentioned above (**3.24**), make for the optimal attitude to *get the elbows connected directly to the middle of our spine,* which constitutes the essential elastic anchoring point, the steady base for a neutral, receiving contact. With suitable elbow attitudes in conjunction with relaxed, 'boneless chicken' forearms and wrists, we can best transfer the horse's forward energy directly from the reins to the seat bones and vice versa (completion of the circuit). The success of this depends on the horse's responsiveness to the driving aids.

3.28 To get the feeling for suitable forearm attitudes, we let the arms dangle down, relaxed by our sides, then raise the forearm until the hand comes up to the correct height (on the line from the elbow to the horse's mouth). Repeat this a number of times – the forearms should feel relaxed and leaden. Another concept is to let the forearm (hand) drop like a rock, from its correct position. This provides a conscious connection with making the forearm be relaxed, even instantly limp, at will – the 'pointy elbow' needs to be elastically maintained while doing this, however, and should not go forward.

3.29 With the understanding of the benefits the above requirements bring, we can imagine how it becomes possible to ride as though

---

12 A useful distinction between 'opening' and 'broadening' contributed by Sue Terrall.
13 See Müseler's *Riding Logic*.

OPPOSITE *Ludwig Koch. Collected walk. Clearly representative of the old standard, 'two-thirds of the horse in front of the rider, one third behind'. Note the presence of the attitudes described in 3.27.*

the horse has no head and neck, and as though we have no upper body. In other words, we end up riding the horse's body predominantly with our seat/body/legs and receive the energy in our elbows (lower back 3.27). Ironically, after having gone through all that effort to acquire correct upper body attitudes, the upper body effectively disappears! This surely applies to many things, the less one is aware of any instrument the better it is.

3.30 Stretching the whole position consolidates our withers, seat bones, and heels, connecting them by the same energy pattern. Once we learn to do so correctly, the stretch becomes like a tangible implement whereby our body becomes bell-like enabling the smallest aids to ring clearly through us and through the whole horse.

3.31 Through maintaining suitable seat/position attitudes we raise the horse up to our steady, balanced correctness. When we carry ourselves, the horses will be able to carry themselves and us more easily. The alternative lowers us down to the horse's undisciplined imbalance and crookedness, which ironically may result in a kind of strange, unwanted 'congruity' in which both horse and rider are comfortable because they are equally unbalanced/crooked. See photographs opposite.

3.32 Just to think of the word 'elegance' is like applying a magic potion which draws all the position aspects into one voice, resulting in a beautiful, practical form. Elegance encompasses elements of both

OPPOSITE

TOP LEFT *The author on Barty. Shoulder-in right at the trot. The rider is not sitting 'square' over the middle of the horse whereby ideal harmony is not present. The horse is leaning in, and the rider is sitting more on the outside half of the horse. See section 3.31.*

TOP RIGHT *White line runs through the horse's center.*

BOTTOM LEFT *Black line runs through the rider's center.*

BOTTOM RIGHT *Here the unsynchronized state becomes clear. To correct this, the rider needs to place more weight on the inside seat bone, and down the inside knee, while rebalancing the horse with a half-halt between the inside leg and the outside rein, then the two lines would merge into one.*

physical and spiritual wholeness – balance, efficiency, ease, nonchalance, self-worth, self-assurance, confidence (these entirely empty of egotism, or arrogance), simplicity, and truthfulness – all qualities of being real.

Attitudes

3.33 The body toned, not tight ... supple, not sloppy.

3.34 The forward desire of our seat and position is that which unifies horse and rider. It is the external purposefulness written in our body which says, 'Let's go *there*'.

3.35 Being forward in the saddle does not mean with the hips or seat bones only. We must have a forward *attitude*, literally, with every cell of our body. The solar plexus must be just as leading in its intention as the hips and seat bones are. That is why leaning back is to be avoided, because the upper body withdraws into a backward attitude in an erroneous attempt to shove the hips and the horse forward.

3.36 Though the seat/position needs to go harmoniously with the horse's movement at the walk, it is important to keep our body all of a piece, and avoid breaking or wobbling loosely in the lower back and hips at each stride (belly flopping). This does not imply that we should be stiff, but we need to assume a regal bearing, to become elastically toned and consolidated, which helps the horse to be balanced and carrying.

3.37 Is it possible to balance a string or a blob of jelly on your finger? Is it possible to balance a riding stick on your finger? That is why the consolidating quality of good posture is so essential, it turns our body into a balanceable unit for the horse.

The hands

3.38 Our hands need to give the horse a steady place to come up to, and on which to work himself off, and become balanced. Yet, they need to be transparent to allow the light of forwardness through. This describes the filtering hand. These effects can only be achieved when appropriately orchestrated in conjunction with animating aids which combine to bring the horse into balance.

3.39 Quietness of the hand does not mean being static; aliveness of the hand does not mean it should fiddle about actively. It needs to become an elastic, living, *relevant* part of the horse. This is achieved through the driving aids – riding our hips and the horse forward through our elbows, in the presence of correct position attitudes, described in **3.24** to **3.28**. This encourages horses to reach for the bridle, whereby they too become a *living* part of the contact, and start to perceive the bridle as their friend, rather than an uncomfortable intruder. Not only does this make it easier for the rider to keep suitable hand qualities and attitudes, but the horses gain joyfulness in their relationship towards the rider and the work. In fact, one could say that in this way the work is transformed into 'the riding game'.

3.40 To acquire the feeling for the above, some riders find it helpful to look down at their hands *briefly,* getting a mental picture of them being quiet relative to the withers, then looking away and, while broadening the front line, concentrating on the feeling of riding their hips through the elbows.

3.41 When looking at a rider's hand from the side, the face of the knuckles should be perpendicular to the ground, and the knuckle of the little finger should generally have a forward attitude towards the horse's mouth. This latter point can be clearly seen in all the illustrations presented in this volume. When the knuckles tend towards being parallel to the ground, the hands automatically assume an inappropriate downward-backward attitude (which is often associated with a conscious or unconscious forcing down of the horse's head).

3.42 We talk about the hand, but we mean the seat/position attitudes. Thus, if we want to use the hand, we should use the seat and leg instead, and we will usually be right.

3.43 To overcome problems in ourselves, do so in the seat/position. To overcome problems in the horse, do so in the hindquarters. These points only operate constructively, however, in the presence of wholesome mental attitudes towards the horse.

Ancillary concepts

3.44 Tai chi, yoga, or the Alexander Technique can be complementary adjuncts to riding, being avenues to help gain control over our bodies, and grow in awareness of how the physical and spiritual interact. They may prove especially useful for riders who have difficulties with coordination or tensions.

Waldimar Seunig. An exemplary, impulsive passage. Horse well in front of the rider. This 'billboard' is telling it like it is. See 5.25, 5.26.

CHAPTER IV

Communication: the Aids

Woo Nature with love and selflessness, and all things will be accomplished in their due season.

THE TEACHINGS OF OSIRIS

Introduction

WHEN COMPARED TO MOST other means of human communication, the rider's 'feeling' language of aiding is indeed unique, its messages being relayed mainly through the tactile senses.

The natural aids can be arranged into four main categories:

- **Weight aids** These are based on the laws of physics to which the horses react instinctively (gravity, dynamic balance, centrifugal force, and movement of mass – overcoming inertia or momentum).

- **Pressure aids** These are made up of leg or rein influences, which rely on the horses' sensitivity to the slightest physical touches or pressures, such as feeling a fly landing on their 'royal' bodies.

- **Vocal aids** These are meant to soothe, or encourage, or on rare occasions to be stern.

- **Psychological aids** These aids are based on the creature's acute perception for things metaphysical: the influences initiated through the rider's thoughts and intentions, coloured by personality, moods or emotions, all of which the horses pick up either ethereally or through sensing the slightest changes that thought power reflects in the rider's body.

Much as with spoken languages, with aiding we can choose to hobble along with a small, anemic vocabulary and broken 'Equinish', or we can expand our treasury of words and brush up on our spelling and grammar, and thus be able to articulate a broader spectrum of concepts, from the most brilliant colours to the subtlest of hues.

Concepts, tools and guidelines for dialogue with the horse

4.1 Language, words, aids, and even rituals are all similar in this regard; they are merely instruments, conveyances, or tubes through which the message they wish to convey can flow. When any one of these becomes more important than its message, it blocks instead of enlightens. Could the same not be said for institutions, societies or, for that matter, individuals; would they too not become a hindrance when they lose sight of their purpose as instruments or vessels, empty of themselves, through which higher truth can flow for the good of all?

4.2 Synonyms for the word 'aids': requests, signals, explanations, directives, guides, indications, encouragements, invitations, and as a verb: to help, to assist, to serve. Some antonyms could be: commands, threats, coercions, forcings, intimidations, demands, orders, and as a verb: to accost, or to violate.

4.3 Among the benefits of basing our aiding on natural law is that, as we become proficient at it, we are able to communicate with almost any horse virtually immediately, whether they have had any training or not.

4.4 As important as they are, technicalities alone will not assure good responses from the horse. But when combined with equestrian tactfulness, a keen sense of timing, and having the right heart toward the matter, then effective, harmonious results become possible.

4.5 Aiding is actually more like singing than speaking, because its effectiveness is so heavily dependent on the quality of its intonation, expressiveness and feeling – the essentials on which melodiousness is built.

4.6 There is a saying in carpentry, 'Let the hammer drive the nail'. So too in riding, we should let the aids inspire the horse to respond as we wish, rather than trying to move the horse's body with our own physical effort. Dance your horse forward, do not push him.

4.7 We must avoid being negatively reactionary, and strive towards positive reinforcement instead. This in no way implies a denial of the actual state of affairs, nor that we should give up the clarity or purpose of our leadership. But it is the rider's calm, dispassionate, unflappable guidance to which horses react best, especially sensitive or nervous ones. In other words we should avoid letting horses know we notice any of their *negative* reactions, or unwanted responses, while simply continuing to show them exactly what we do want, and reinforcing suitable responses with immediate praise.

4.8 With intelligence and tactfulness we can convert difficulties into advantages. For instance, when a horse is a world-class tourist – is readily distracted by things in the environment – all we need to do is *distract* him with the insistent clarity of our aids, making them as persistent and rapid-fire as necessary to achieve the desired results. This redirects the horse's mind constructively toward our purpose. This approach will not work, however, if we lack consistency or resolve, or if we become annoyed and harden our heart against the horse. To use our aids as a weapon of retaliation or punishment, instead of the clear, enabling directives they ought to be, is hardly productive.

4.9 Negative requests, those that start with 'No', or 'Don't', are difficult for the horse to understand. Making our requests in a positive vein, however, such as: 'Look *this* way (into the school)', instead of saying, 'Don't look out the door!'; or saying, 'Come on, stay out on this circle' or, 'Stay off this leg', instead of, 'Don't cut in!', usually achieves better results. Reason? The one is tainted by judgement, the other is a simple, unaffected, doable request. Like us humans, horses do not operate particularly well under the gun of negative or judgemental attitudes.

4.10 It might even be better to think in terms of making 'adjustments' rather than 'corrections'. Adjustments are emotionless changes, whereas the concept of making corrections implies judgement … something is 'wrong'. Well, horses have no sense of morality, therefore they are not wrong, though they might not be doing exactly what we wish.

4.11 When horses do not respond exactly as we have intended, we simply need to ask again, in a matter-of-fact, emotionally neutral way and, if necessary, with greater clarity or intensity show them exactly what we do want, without even a hint of resentment, annoyance or anger in our aiding voice.

4.12 Just as a well-made saddle fits the horse's back, and a well-made shoe fits the hoof – and not the other way around – so too the aiding influences we impart must fit the horse and the circumstances at any given moment.

4.13 Aiding could be compared to colouring: a little green, a little blue – add just a tinge of yellow – there, that is just right! Or, perfect aiding could be seen as a straight line to the goal. In practice, our actual aid might be more or less left or right of this imaginary ideal centerline. The beginner tends to make exaggerated corrections, swinging from extreme left to extreme right, and only briefly and accidentally hits 'just right' as the center is crossed. The advanced rider also goes from left to right, but, through experience, is better able to adjust the aids quickly and deftly to the needs of the moment, and therefore generally hovers closer to the aiding sweet spot.

4.14 If we breathe the aids into the horse, it helps us to stay relaxed and keeps the communicative lines of feeling open between the horse and rider. This is especially significant when stronger aids may occasionally need to be given.

4.15 Though it is indeed important to be able to aid exactly and independently with just one seat bone, leg, or hand, it is essential that we 'live' our intention unambiguously with every cell of our body. It becomes an expression not unlike pantomime (not in an *overt* sense, of course).

4.16 Horses are like water, they go where the energy required to do a task is least. Therefore, if they escape our aiding, it is not necessarily a sign of willful disobedience. They are just living in accordance with their nature: they are comfortable in their crookedness and laziness. However, if we can tactfully bar every option but our own, making *our* way the path of least resistance, the horses will usually follow it gladly. In this way we achieve our goals relatively effortlessly while avoiding confrontation.

4.17 That which we think of an aid as being, is what the horse will recognize it to be. This applies, for example, to the threefold function of the inside leg: either driving, yielding, or emphasized as the passive post around which we bend the horse. These can be used individually, or combined to work almost simultaneously (**6.11**).

4.18 If we are visionary – thinking, preparing and acting ahead – we seem to have all the time in the world. If we tend towards being reactionary, however, our aiding usually comes just that bit too late, leaving us constantly scurrying about playing catch-up. We relinquish our leadership because of this.

4.19 If we only look and think ahead, we cannot learn from our mistakes. If we only look back, we are parked cars and the horse has no leader. We fare best by living in the eternal present through what we 'feel' under us, while basing our purposeful, forward-thinking decisions on experience from the past (**3.4**).

4.20 *What* we ask for defines our leadership. *When* we ask for it, *how* we ask for it, and *how much* we ask for, that must be determined by the horses' nature and their individual needs at any given moment.

4.21 The *what* of our leadership entails that we determine: **a)** the **gait** (purity, balance, and exact length of stride); **b)** the **school figure** (which kind, and exact size and location); **c)** the **exercise** (a judicious combination of the first two which makes up the gymnastic aspects of riding).

4.22 When we lack purpose we can easily annoy or dull the horse by aimlessly picking at the poor creature. This can best be overcome by always aiding with a clear external purpose ('Let's go *there*', in the chosen gait, school figure, exercise); and learning to adjust the pattern and sequence of the external exercise until the internal horse feels better under us.

4.23 Though we can certainly have a forward-generating effect from the seat, we can no more push the horse forward with an *active* seat than we can pick ourselves up by our socks. The seat's influence, though very real, should be absolutely quiet relative to the horse's back, and other than its good effects on the horse, it should be invisible to the observer.

4.24 Useful forward urgency in the horse must be awakened through tactful driving. Indiscreet whacking or spurring only results in tension – a response based on fear or resentment instead of understanding.

OPPOSITE

ABOVE *Richard Wätjen, working canter on the snaffle.*

BELOW *Richard Wätjen, collected canter on the double bridle. Regarding these two photos, Wätjen pointed out that one of the technical differences between the working canter and collected canter can be readily discerned by the distance between the diagonal pair of legs, the second phase of the canter sequence (in this case the left hind and the right front).*

4.25 How can we best maintain an adequate level of energy in horses without having to drive them constantly? The answer lies in delegating. To delegate we must have a clear purpose in mind, deciding *exactly* how much forward energy we want, and converting that into balance through the half-halt principle (**5.32** to **5.38**).[1] If we lack clarity, consistency, or resolve, or are asleep at the switch half the time, we will not succeed. While keeping good position attitudes in mind, we must engage our seat and effectively use our legs (backed up by the stick or spurs if necessary) to animate the horse, and literally bring him up to a forward energy level of, let us say, 8, on a scale from 1 to 10. We absolutely *must show* the horse exactly what we mean by that 8. Then, other than providing a small shadow aid (**4.32**), we must leave the horse alone, that is, until his energy level drops below 7, at which time we must remind him of his task by saying, 'Hey, down there, come on, you get back up to 8', and then leave him alone again. If we are consistent, the horses will begin to recognize that they are left alone as long as they maintain their energy level between 7 and 8. And because horses love to be left alone by the rider, they will begin to seek out that quiet place on their own, where we continue to encourage them with the gentle shadow aid and praise them for their wonderful contribution. Needless to say, the principle of delegating applies to all aiding concepts. It gives horses the space to figure things out for themselves, the confidence to act, and nurtures their desire to contribute.

4.26 The sequence of the rider's aiding influences is: a) first, get the *passive* elegance of the 'zero' position attitudes well organized (**3.17**)[2]: i.e. rest vertically, independently balanced; open front line by raising ribcage; fill nape of neck (raise your withers **3.25**); hang shoulders naturally back and down; **b)** then, *if the horse accepts our presence in the saddle* (is calm, driveable), add the more positive, though still passive, seat/position influences as needed, these are: broaden the front line; 'tip the chair'[3]; ride the horse and hips

---

1 *Dressage Formula*, 3rd Ed., 060, 'The Half-halt'.
2 *Dressage Formula*, 3rd Ed. See all the details of the correct position, Chapter 2.
3 See Müseler, *Riding Logic*.

through the elbows, and the chest through the shoulders; 'feel' the seat bone energy over the knees (kneeling attitude); passive increases of leg pressure can now be used; c) if more response is needed, introduce *active* leg aids; d) finally, if necessary, reinforce the *active* leg aids with stick or spurs. Each one of these points is progressively layered on the previous one(s). Point d) for example, should only come into play when the other points a), b), and c) are already duly engaged. It is vital to measure just the right proportion of these elements to suit each horse and circumstance. Note Though the various details in point b) are mentioned separately, they are actually just facets of one energy pattern — that of engaging our seat/position in order to animate the horse.

4.27 Once the horse has responded to either the stick or spur, we must avoid giving that *extra* aid 'just for good measure'. Not only does it tend to extinguish the horse's willingness, but it often justifiably raises the horse's ire.

4.28 It is essential to drive only when horses are in an accepting state. If they are not, we must *rest* … and *wait* … passively … and only if and when they accept again (are calm, driveable, not tense or rushing), judiciously re-introduce the driving aids (5.47): drive a bit, get a response, coast a bit.

4.29 The same applies to training in general, that we work horses carefully within their *acceptance zone* where they can understand and partake. Outside of that zone we fail to achieve higher standards because the horses are no longer in a state to be able to (or wish to) contribute willingly. When the aiding is either too brief, too small, lacks clarity, determination, or purpose, it has little or no useful effect. When the aiding is too long, too strong, or too aggressively applied, a disconnection between horse and rider occurs, whereby the aids (though the horse might even respond to them) do not go *through* the horse; they are in fact rejected by the horses at a deeper level, and go around the outside of them. Egon von Neindorff would warn, "Bring the horse up to the highest limit, but don't push him over it".

4.30 We should strive to refine our work to the point where decimals (.01, 2.7, or .34) are sufficient to have the horse respond, and not always aid with whole numbers. When we have it right, the distinction between our request and the horse's response begins to fade. They seem to merge into one and the same act, and the horse seems to be connected directly to our mind.

4.31 We should avoid getting into 'common labourer' mode, and endeavour to stay in 'independent assistant' mode instead. If we cannot just sit there most of the time (with the exception of a small shadow aid), we are simply doing too much.

4.32 A shadow aid is a small, passive, maintaining influence, an encouraging presence which helps the horse to know that he was good to respond to our last aid, and that he should continue to do that. For example: the active aid says, 'Come on, go more forward!', then, as the horse responds, the shadow aid softly whispers, 'There, good boy, that's right, continue on just like that . . .' The shadow aid is technically made up of the 'maintaining seat', (**4.26, b**)[4] but more importantly it is represented by our continued *mental* focus on our purpose, whereby the horse is not left in a leaderless vacuum during the periods in between our active aids.

4.33 Hold nothing. Live by the quantum theory of aid giving, imparting little lumps of aiding energy: Aid – f-l-o-w. Re-aid – f-l-o-w ... ad infinitum. Hold ***nothing!***

4.34 Preventing is similarly to be avoided. It is just another form of holding. Instead, we need to allow horses to make their mistakes honestly (just for a split second, or so) and *only then* correct them by showing them again exactly what we do want. Let this cycle happen again and again, until they start to make (or maintain) the right choice on their own. On the other hand, it is helpful to make timely preventive corrections (weeding before they take over the garden; repainting the house before it gets shabby) as opposed to

---

[4] *Dressage Formula*, 3rd Ed., 022.

being constantly in a preventing (holding) state (never putting the hoe or paint brush down just in case …).

4.35 We must dare to lose what we have gained, and patiently set about refinding it repeatedly. *Only by daring to release (or neutralize) after each aid,* trusting in the horse's intelligence and generosity, will we ultimately have what we want without either fearfully or ambitiously having to hang onto it. Adjust them, then trust them! We are indeed liberated when we free ourselves of all attachment.

4.36 It is helpful to see 'losing what we have gained' in a positive light. It is that which spurs us on to gain more thorough experience with finding the path between having and not having – doing so a thousand times, until we become so sure of every detail of the path that we can find the way to our goal blindfolded.

4.37 To perpetuate what we have achieved, it is best to think in terms of a 'refreshment rate' of aiding, getting the necessary little resolutions to each request. For example, we need to refresh the horse's balance before it is lost, likewise for the bend, or the horse's carriage, or the canter; or we can deliberately make small changes of bend, position alterations, or transitions. Such refreshment can be as frequent as necessary to help the performance become steady, while avoiding any hint of holding. This is central to keeping horse and rider independent, supple, and interactively attuned over extended periods.

4.38 This concept cannot be sufficiently repeated, understood, or practiced, it is the very life-breath of effective aiding: 'Give an aid – get a response – stop giving the aid', but remember **4.32**.

4.39 We should strive to speak as softly as possible, while listening as loudly as possible – having a huge elephant ear on every aid we give, straining to hear the slightest responses from the horse *while aiding,* so we can immediately stop giving the aid as we should. We are best able to 'listen' (that is, 'feel') when mentally and physically relaxed.

4.40 Being feeling and working with care is good, being irresolute, gingerly or hesitant is not. Being decisive and effective is good, being arrogant, aggressive, or inconsiderate is not.

4.41 *All aiding must be given from a basis of 'two-sidedness'.* This *passive* equality is made up of feeling that the weight of both legs/heels/feet is even down through the stirrups (this evenness is not relative to the horse, but relative to the ground: the legs being like two plumb lines to the center of the earth); feeling both seat bones even and central in the saddle; feeling both pillars (3.10) even above the seat bones; feeling both shoulders hanging back and down evenly through the elbows; feeling both reins even, with the hands held evenly above the withers. For concepts on how to find evenness in our *influences,* see **4.44, 6.25, 6.27**.

4.42 **Diagonal** aids straighten the horse: the leg (seat bone!) on the side of the evading croup, the rein (seat bone!) on the side of the evading shoulder. The same principle can also be used deliberately to set the horse up in the two-track positions. Good control over the seat bones is essential (3.10 to 3.13). **Note** Even if we are riding on a straight line, and deliberately have no bend in our horse, it is essential always to choose which is our inside and outside, doing so simply by having a *little* emphasis on our own diagonal aiding influence: just being aware of feeling '*Inside seat bone*' ... '*outside shoulder nicely back and down*' will do the job

4.43 **Unilateral** aids stem sideways drifting off the intended school figure: leg (seat bone!) and rein on the same side. This concept can also be used deliberately for leg-yielding. For **4.42**, and **4.43**, the leg is the main *active* initiator of the requests or adjustments; the rein is usually only to be passively confirmed (just thinking of it is usually enough) – *it is essential that this 'confirming' does not alter the bend in the neck.*

4.44 If both half-halting and straightening entail the use of diagonal aiding, what is the difference between them? For straightening, one would use *greater pressure* in the active leg (on the side of the evading croup) and its diagonal rein partner (on the side of the evading shoulder). For half-halting (or halting), there must be *equal pressure* in both legs and *equal pressure* in both reins; though the inside leg or the outside rein may, if necessary, be made active, the pressure is to remain even. Remember, either active leg or active rein, not both active simultaneously. An important detail regarding this subject is that one could substitute the words 'equal pressure' with 'equal *value*' or 'equal *influence*' instead (**6.26**).

4.45 What is the most basic difference between leg-yielding and driving? For driving, both legs must have *equal* pressure. For leg-yielding, the leg from which we want the horse to yield must have *greater* pressure than the other. However, we must always gently hug the horse between both legs during leg-yielding – the leg from which we want the horse to yield asks, the other leg, though lighter, gently receives. For suitable leg positioning see **6.11** to **6.14**.

4.46 For guidance, balance (half-halt), and straightness we need to think inside leg AND outside rein. For turns on the forehand, circle increase, leg-yielding, or shoulder-in we need to think inside leg TO outside rein.

4.47 The 'inside leg *and* outside rein' concept comprises three major influences: **a)** it establishes the balance; **b)** it improves straightness; **c)** it makes the guiding aids efficient and operable.

4.48 The most misused aid is the inside rein. The most neglected aid is the outside leg. This latter point is not surprising, since the outside seat bone is also often weak and neglected (being either lighter, or lagging behind). This may be caused by an overbearing focus being put on the inside seat bone at the expense of the outside one (**4.41**).

4.49 Force elicits counter-force. If we want to overcome the horse's tensions or resistance, it works wonders to emulate water ... softness overcomes hardness. "A soft answer turns away wrath, but a harsh word stirs up anger."[5] The following point provides an example.

---

5 Proverbs. 15: 1, New King James Version, (Nashville, Tennessee: Thomas Nelson, Inc.) 1982. (Oak Harbor, WA: Logos Research Systems, Inc.) 1994.

4.50 If the horse resists against the hand, we should avoid trying to keep the head down with a stark, hard, downward-boring, or backward-working hand (it is fine to *allow* the hands to be low under such circumstances, but it is essential that they are absolutely neutral in that low position). Instead, in the presence of an open front line, the hand needs to assume a steady place, and yet not be stark or blocking (3.14, 3.41, 3.43, 5.30), as the driving aids encourage the horse to reach into that contact. Rather than trying to get the nose down (or 'in'), *think* of stretching the mane towards the poll by way of a solid, forward, working gait instead. If the horse should speed up, the half-halt will regain the balance/rhythm, after which we must 'give while driving' again. Repeat as necessary. The horse will soon settle in and begin to reach independently and elastically for the bridle once again.

4.51 Hindquarters engaged equals shoulders free. Horses need our assistance to learn to carry their shoulders in the buoyant, forward energy of their hindquarters. Pushing our hands forward toward the horse's mouth, like pushing a 'tea trolley'[6] in front of us (not away from us) as we drive, without losing the contact, helps to achieve this end. This is especially effective when done immediately after a half-halt.

4.52 Use bright, crisp, 'hot potato' aids for dull horses – creamy, smooth, refined aids for nervous or sensitive horses.

4.53 To achieve the desirable 'potato in a sock' attitude, we need to surround (gently hug, or snuggle close to) our horse within the continuous, neutral, passive, elastic presence of our riding instruments: the seat, legs and reins. This constitutes effective framing.[7] The undesirable opposite to this happens when, for lack of forwardness in the horse, and/or our inability to establish a continuous contact with our seat bones, reins, and legs, the horse becomes a 'marble in

---

6 Egon von Neindorff.
7 *Dressage Formula*, 3rd Ed., 038.

a can' and rattles around loosely and uncontrolledly – bouncing from wall to wall, so to speak – between our aiding tools.

4.54 What may the hand do? **a)** Half-halt deliberately; **b)** bend or straighten deliberately; **c)** passive guidance. All else is unwanted 'fiddling' which usually only has one specious agenda: to achieve the *symptom* of getting or keeping the horse's head down in position. **Note** After each of the above three points we need to repeat the refrain, 'While *always* addressing the whole horse with our seat/position and legs as necessary!'

4.55 The rein aids must be at the *end* of the aiding system, not the beginning. They are largely meant to receive and direct the energy which is already naturally offered by the horse, or generated by our driving aids. Accordingly, all rein aids must be well supported in (they must be overcome by) adequate forward energy in the horse; this can only be achieved in the presence of predominant, well-suited seat/position/leg attitudes (this does *not* mean that we need continuous *active* aiding).

4.56 Isn't it amazing how horses usually go better immediately when the hand becomes incapacitated because the rider has put both reins into one hand! (**6.25, 6.27, 6.28**).

4.57 We could see the hand as nothing more than an innocent bystander, a witness to the state of the horse, as opposed to being a central figure. Only those who have learned to truly appreciate this through years of earnest practice, know how devilishly difficult it is for the hand to play its refined, passive role – its ability to do *nothing* – well! The old adage 'less is more' certainly applies.

Two sides of the coin ... the extremes

4.58 **For timid riders** Horses need and respect leadership. The most essential aspect of our being the leader of the partnership is to have clarity of purpose, and to be decisive in carrying out our objective, even if we do not feel entirely sure or competent. We must make up

Tête de Cheval blanc. *Théodore Géricault (1791–1824). Musée de Louvre, Paris.*

our mind, put our program into the computer, and go for it! To fulfill this, it is crucial to get responses from our aids right *now*, today, however crude or inept we might initially be. Because only when we begin to get some kind of a response (large enough that we ourselves notice it!) *from each and every request* will we then, through practice, gradually improve the way in which we achieve those responses. When we are hesitant, indecisive, or irresolute, the horses either ignore us or quickly take over the decision-making role, which is seldom a pleasant or useful experience.

4.59 **For strong, confident riders** If we could but realize the strength that lies in *benevolent* leadership, which gives space to those we are leading to be themselves – and when serenity rules our hearts – a whole new world of perspective, feeling, and experience would open up to us. It enables us to truly listen to the horse's needs, and gives us the composure and confidence to let the water of time develop the seedlings of the creature's willing contributions, so they can grow naturally into beautiful plants and blossoms. We can no more succeed in forcing a horse to produce the deep beauty of true *elastic,* balanced work, than we can force an oak sapling to become a glorious, tall shade tree in a few short years. We can only diminish ourselves and regrettably damage the horse when we are impatient and disrespectful, and end up giving-in to our negative emotions, or to our greedy, self-serving ambitions. Our task is called leadership, not dictatorship. The horse is our conscience ...

Sally Cleaver's Andalusian stallion, Banbury Sampson. A wonderfully impulsive extended trot showing exemplary, natural, 'uphill' balance – sheer exuberance in motion!

CHAPTER V

Training Concepts

He comes into the arena on two horses, and rides out on one.
OBERBEREITER JOHANN MEIXNER of the
Spanish Riding School, commenting on his pupil, Richard Wätjen.[1]

Introduction

HORSES SHOW US through their demeanour whether our interaction with them makes them feel secure and content, or unsettled and frightened.[2] But even after twenty years of perfect training they still never know *why* things feel better ... or worse. This is because their way of thinking is largely reactionary, rather than more visionary, conceptual, or deductive such as ours can be. As remarkable as horses appear to be at solving certain problems, when they feel ungainly under saddle, it would never occur to them to deduce, 'Oh, I know what's wrong, I feel a bit unbalanced, so if I generate more forward energy from my hindquarters, I'll regain my balance and feel better again!' Instead, the creatures live very much in the present and are inclined to react either to the stimuli of internal biological needs or to external events happening in their

---

[1] Waldimar Seunig, *Meister der Reitkunst*, Erich Hoffmann Verlag, 1960. p95.
[2] *Dressage Formula*, 3rd Ed., sections 068 to 071.

immediate environment. In nature, for example, they might go energetically and nicely balanced – showing off their spectacular stuff – only when excited by a clap of thunder, or when wolves threaten the herd, or out of sheer joy in life which may spark the herd to gallop and buck playfully on a crisp, autumn morning.

Other than such instances the horses tend to just plop along lazily on the forehand, with minimal effort, over to the next clump of grass for a little lunch. It is nature's perfect efficiency, to use energy only when absolutely necessary. In light of this, the significance of the rider's incitement to ignite the horse's forward urge can not be overstated – it is the very life-blood of horsemanship. *The clarity of the rider's intention, motivated by will, becomes the horse's reason to act.*

An avenue of approach

5.1 Awakening plenty of forward energy is like building a good, hefty fire to heat a house ... without burning it down, of course.

5.2 Though in Latin *equilibrium* means 'equally weighted', in the equestrian sense we could think of it as 'equally free' ... especially mentally and emotionally, without which physical freedom is not possible. All the more reason why the horse must not be forced if true horsemanship is to be achieved.

5.3 When we assume full responsibility for the act of riding, the joy of experiencing harmony based on mutual participation becomes possible. But the moment we put the onus on the horse, however subtly, the lines are drawn, the battle begins, and true horsemanship leaves the scene.

5.4 The Hippocratic Oath embodies concepts that can be readily adopted into our equestrian ideals. To paraphrase several points: "First, do no harm!"; and, "... always be helpful; do all for the good of the patient [horse]".[3]

5.5 If it is good for the horse, it is always good for the rider. The converse is not necessarily true.

5.6 Faith and trust in the horse's intelligence, generosity and ability, bring rich rewards. Unbelief and distrust beget precisely what they anticipate: noncompliance, and untrustworthiness.

5.7 Training or adjusting the horse operate on a principle of *momentary,* and *slight,* exaggeration. It is somewhat like overbending a coat-hanger wire, just a little, so that when it is released it remains bent just right on its own. For example, a horse who is prone to rushing would be worked deliberately more slowly; a horse who is lazy would be ridden more briskly, etc. Needless to say, such exaggerations should be used only briefly. We need to get to the center (normal aiding and responses) as soon as possible.

5.8 Good riding and training hinges on finding the key for each lock we meet. Of course, we could enter by force, and sadly that option is used all too frequently. This is exactly the critical 'Y' in the road where other methods and mentalities part ways from the classical path. Because the true horseman will not even entertain the idea of forced entry just to satisfy some preconceived notion about what horses should do or be. Only when we approach them with dignity and respect, and let the resourcefulness, clarity, and consistency of our technique be guided by appropriate attitudes, will the horses respond with confidence, based on understanding instead of fear.

5.9 It takes much experience to be able to differentiate between **a)** the suitability of briefly asserting our leadership with a few emphatic aids, backed up by stick or spur if necessary, and **b)** the tyranny of forcing horses to do work which is unsuitable for their level or, worse yet, coercing them to take on attitudes which are injurious to their nature. Here, truth and falsity appear to lie side by side. Yet, for the connoisseur it is like trying to compare glass with diamonds, or ormolu with gold – they are, simply put, irreconcilable.

---

3 Excerpts from 'The Oath', By Hippocrates, a.k.a: 'The Hippocratic Oath'. Written 400 B.C.E. Translated by Francis Adams.

5.10 Punishment should be resorted to extremely rarely. On the other hand, discipline is necessary, being a benign, intelligent refocusing, rechanneling, redirecting of energies towards a noble goal: to enhance, rather than diminish. Discipline is the basis for all improvement for both horse and rider.

5.11 Fine horsemanship is based on maintaining a kind heart toward horses, and keeping their best interest ever in mind even when, like a child, they may occasionally need a firmer hand of guidance. In the end, when well handled, the truth of their lovely willingness and eager compliance shines through and we feel deeply moved and uplifted by the heartwarming encounter.

5.12 Each day again, horses need to be given time to settle in, mentally and physically, to accept our presence in the saddle before we can expect them to respond favourably. Walking 'on the buckle' for about five minutes before taking up any rein contact usually achieves the desired results. If we want to enter into their sovereign territory, we need to be patient and polite, and to our unexpected joy, the horses will soon invite us in for afternoon tea, because they are curious and gregarious and love the company of good friends.

5.13 Irrespective of the level of training, a thoughtful warm-up, consisting of simple, free-flowing, working gaits and large, open school figures, is a vital foundation for all work each day again.

5.14 Training entails the nurturing of good habits through thoughtful, consistent conditioning. Though a certain amount of repetition may be necessary, prolonged grinding on one exercise is usually not helpful.

5.15 Fairly frequent changing of rein is also significant, and brings better results than lengthy working on one hand. This approach is all part of sound gymnastics that helps develop ambidexterity in both horse and rider. We want to strike a happy medium though, between too little changing, whereby things become stale, and changing so frequently that it upsets the smoothness or continuity of the work.

5.16 Dancing partners would not find harmony if either one were to concentrate solely on the other, aside from feeling a peripheral awareness of each other's presence, that is. But when having their minds, their senses, attuned to the rhythm, the feel, the expression of the music – a 'third person' outside them both – they are naturally drawn together into harmony. Similarly, riders need to think mainly of the work: **a)** feeling, *counting*, getting into the even, dancing rhythm of the gait; **b)** while guiding the horse on the school figure of choice; **c)** doing some beneficial exercise. These, combined, are the external purpose which represent the third person for horse and rider, and draws them together in harmony. As an added bonus, it is one of the finest ways of automatically keeping the horse's mind on the *work* instead of on other things, or strictly on 'the rider'; to engender the horses' willing contribution, we want to get their minds on our purpose, not on us. Feel what's under you, think of what's out there (4.20, 4.21).

5.17 It is far more effective to get the horse's mind on the work by saying, 'Do this ... [specific request]', something as simple as, 'Look this way', rather than saying empty, purposeless things like, 'Listen to *me!*', or, 'Pay attention!'

5.18 Good work always shows itself by horses reaching evenly and continuously into both reins. If they lighten up on one side, we need to drive them up more with the seat bone and leg on that lighter side. If the contact becomes empty on both sides, driving (with equal pressure on both sides) will reconfirm the horse's honest presence in both reins. If the horse leans on both reins, then simply re-animating with the driving aids and rebalancing with a half-halt, or riding some transitions, will lighten the horse into better self-carriage once again. The criteria for the correct head position of the horse is: **a)** the poll must be the highest point; **b)** the face should be at or slightly in front of the vertical; and **c)** the horse's ears must be on the same level.[4]

---

4 *Dressage Formula*, 3rd Ed., 042 to 044, see especially the italicized text on p68.

5.19 'If the horse isn't reaching, you're not driving'. (However, keep in mind 4.28.)

5.20 We want the horse not only to reach for the bridle, but to step into and go *through* it. Needless to say, this has nothing to do with running away against or behind the bit. When the work is right, we get a wonderfully elastic, 'compressible' feeling between the seat and the hand, as though the reins were looped around a large beach balloon, as the horse goes confidently forward.

5.21 Sometimes the obvious needs to be stated: the requirement of needing to have the horse always reaching into *both* reins equally, implies into the *inside* rein as well. Unless horses continually reach for (and gently accept) the inside rein as well as the outside one, they are not correctly 'on the aids'. A clarification follows.

5.22 To be able to give up the contact on the inside rein for a stride or two, might be considered evidence that the horse is independently balanced and soft to the bend. When this concept is taken to an extreme, however, and we begin to ride whole circles with a slack inside rein, we effectively teach horses a trick through which they learn to contract or reserve their energy on the inside. An artificial bend, carriage and lightness result, and subsequent difficulty demonstrating the *sine qua non* of excellent work: correct forward and downward stretching with the nose in front of the vertical.

5.23 Constantly fiddling or sawing with the hands to get and keep horses' heads down, does not belong to worthy horsemanship. If we learn to control the horses' energy rather than their bodies, they will consequently begin to carry and thus 'form' *themselves* into the highly coveted external shape.

5.24 It is so dearly important that we dedicate ourselves to search for substantial causes which will bear genuine results, as opposed to chasing after baseless symptoms.

5.25 We could see the position and attitudes of horses' heads and necks as their natural 'billboards' with which they clearly advertise their assessment of the way things are going. When we allow only the horses to write on the billboard it remains a valid guideline for us. However, as soon as we start scribbling on the billboard ourselves, through any artificial placement of the head and neck, we run into falsity and shut down a horse's say.

5.26 If we are sincere about following classical principles, we would be eager to let horses have their vote. Because if we do something inappropriate, we could then be genuinely delighted, instead of chagrined or irritated, when a horse points this out by going up against the bridle, or does not bend, or gets too light and comes behind the hand. After all, if we were to listen to these instructions from horses, understanding they are merely saying, 'I'm out of balance', or 'My hind legs are not engaging equally', or 'I can't move freely because of the attitude of your hand; or because the proportion between the amount of your hand relative to the amount of your seat/leg is out of kilter' (the hand being usually too strong), not only would we be learning how to ride properly from true masters, the horses themselves, but it would be a wonderfully inexpensive lesson to boot, much cheaper than attending clinics! We can rely implicitly on this one thing: if we become adept at working within the laws of the horses' nature, they will *always* write wonderful things on their billboards. Furthermore, though only very simple work might be demonstrated, the beauty of a horse moving naturally well under a sensitive, harmonious rider is tirelessly enjoyable to experience and to watch.

5.27 We must not confuse the horse's reaching with what might be resistance or leaning. We must not confuse lightness with what might be a lack of genuine reaching (dropping the contact, or 'sucking back' 5.19). Though neither one is desirable, of the two evils, it is better to have the horse somewhat against the hand than artificially light behind it.

5.28 When work lacks in true forwardness, it is characteristic for the horse to vacillate constantly between going either up against the bit or dropping behind it.

Collected trot. Showing fine 'uphill' qualities with great ease, and good, unified, 'diagonal' stepping. From Le Maneige Royal, Antoine de Pluvinel (1555–1620). *J. A Allen.*

5.29 When the horse comes behind the bit (poll low, face behind the vertical) this can best be overcome by lowering our hands, and helping the horse to reach better 'up into the bridle' with the driving aids (supported with a tap of the stick, if necessary!), in conjunction with a rebalancing half-halt (maintain rhythm) and then the giving hand. The common error of raising the hand, or giving sharp upward jerks, does not address the root of the problem: lack of energy and balance.

5.30 Any time we need to counteract the horse's resistance, if we 'sustain' the contact within the presence of good seat/position attitudes, we will not smother the animation but will help to redirect it into the flame of balance instead (3.24 to 3.28).

5.31 'Feathering' the rein is a fine way to dissolve minor one-sided rein resistance which usually occurs on the inside rein. One could say, feathering takes the wind out of the horse's stiff-side sails. We do so by briefly softening or releasing the contact slightly by opening the fingers (without losing contact), and then gently returning the hand/fingers to where they were before the release. Such 'feathering' is most effective when the rider sends the horse nicely forward and *thinks* predominantly of the inside leg and the outside rein. When a horse responds to this by softening the body at the inside leg (this has nothing to do with leg-yielding), we can then easily bend him to the desired degree. Tempting though it may be, bending should not be forced with a powerful, active inside rein. This is because the horse's *apparent* one-sided resistance seldom has to do with stubbornness, and is usually merely a symptom of the hind legs not being equally or adequately engaged. This can be best overcome through suitable forward riding (watch the rhythm) while paying close attention to good seat/position/leg attitudes. The pressure or intensity of the bending aid on the inside rein should be strictly limited to that amount which the horse *willingly* follows (2.13, 6.10 to 6.16; see especially 6.32 and 6.37).

The half-halt [5]

5.32 A half-halt is mainly a rebalancing tool.

5.33 Every rebalancing should encompass straightening. Every straightening should encompass rebalancing.

5.34 Every half-halt implies the need for greater animation. Egon von Neindorff says, "Drive - receive (sustain, or 'take up' the energy) - become lighter again".

5.35 During the half-halt we must bring the seat (horse) up to the hand (bit), not the other way around.

5.36 If response to the half-halt is not crisp, the horse is likely not adequately up to the bridle in forwardness.

5.37 *If an active half-halt is necessary, use the '**Close** - o-p-e-n' concept with the fingers on the outside rein (take note, this is exactly the opposite to 'feathering', 5.31). It is especially important to end up with the 'open', that is, a giving attitude in the hand. Furthermore, the 'close' is to be brief, and the 'o-p-e-n' longer and slower.[6] Always consider suitable seat/position attitudes when half-halting.*

5.38 For the half-halt: either active hand, or active leg, not both *active* simultaneously.

Timing

5.39 To develop a refined sense for the timing of our aids, we must become aware of *feeling* the horse's back moving forward alternately under each half of the seat at the moment the horse's hind leg pushes off the ground on that side. However, we should *not* try to emphasize that motion by adding to it with any extra,

---

5 *Dressage Formula*, 3rd Ed., 060, 'The Half-halt'.
6 Useful detail contributed by Herman Koopmans.

alternating, one-sided *seat* activity which would only disturb the horse. Instead, just be aware of it by simply *feeling* it happen, while maintaining the general intention of having both seat bones with equal forward pressure constantly into the front of the saddle.

5.40 The timing for the *active* driving aid is: during the *last* half of the weight-bearing phase of each hind leg (alternately), and up until, and including, the moment that leg pushes off the ground. Using the walk and the horse's inside hind leg for the example, we would give the driving aid with our inside leg as we *feel* the horse's back going all the way forward under the inside seat; which corresponds to that moment of 'pushing-off' of the hind leg on that side. This, incidentally, is also valid timing for the canter aid. With regard to points 5.40 to 5.43, we can also detect the timing for the aid by feeling for the horse's ribcage 'filling' against our leg, but personally I believe it is better to develop the feel for correct timing with the seat. Incidentally, this discussion is only about suitable timing, and in no way implies the need to use such aids constantly at each and every stride.

5.41 The timing for the *active* half-halt on the outside rein is: just as the inside hind leg strikes the ground, and during the *first* half of the weight-bearing phase of that leg. At the walk, for example, we would give the half-halt on the outside rein as we *feel* the horse's back going all the way forward under the outside seat.

5.42 The timing for the leg-yielding aid is: during the entire forward swinging phase of the horse's corresponding hind leg. For example, when the rider is yielding the horse *from* the right leg, the aid can be given during the entire time when the horse's right hind leg is off the ground.

5.43 The timing for the traverse (half-pass) aid: during the entire time the horse's outside hind leg is off the ground. In this case, the rider's outside leg gives the lateral aid.

5.44 The firing order for exercises aimed at improving lateral leg responsiveness (turns on the forehand, leg-yielding, shoulder-in,

Margot Huelke on Lipizzaner stallion Pluto (Pluto III x Bonita III, Temple Farms bred), ca. 1985. Working trot, 10 meter circle right. Good basic, unified, diagonal movement. Fine, practical position and attitudes of the rider. See sections 5.51, 5.52. Photo by Alston Wolf.

half-pass) is: Halt. Angle. Flow. Take note, these are consecutive, not concurrent. Only when the horse listens to the half-halt (*halt*), and is therefore better balanced, will he respond more easily to the lateral leg aid (*angle*), after which we must go with the horse freely in the direction of the chosen lateral movement (*flow*). Avoid using the lateral leg aid at the same time as the half-halt.

5.45 Animation, straightness, and maintaining the music of the steady, rhythmic beat of the gait, are central to achieving balanced harmony between horse and rider.

5.46 Some thoughts about achieving balance: for rushing horses, 'Slow, but go'; for lazy horses, 'Go, but slow'. In either case, this is not meant to be a simultaneous, contradictory aiding, but, rather, an alternating back and forth between the two.

5.47 When a horse is tense and jigs at the walk: we must *melt* our seat (extra mozzarella), and *ooze* the walk out into longer, smoother strides with the seat and broad front line. If it is a serious case, we need to settle down to the idea of just walking such a horse 'on the buckle' for any number of days, using fairly small voltes at first, until the horse becomes more trusting and settles down *without needing to use the reins* (other than for simple guidance). Trying to slow the horse with the reins, or half-halting is not of value until the horse is calm and allows himself to be driven. Endless patience is indispensable to success, and sharp aids entirely unhelpful. When the horse becomes driveable again, and *if* he needs to be driven, begin doing so by thinking of passively 'emptying a tube of toothpaste' out the front with both legs, while 'tipping the chair'.[7] The use of a few steps of *gentle* leg-yielding may also be a helpful adjunct to such concepts. Generally, just enjoying the time with such nervous, high-strung horses without having any kind of expectation or agenda will bring better results sooner than any so-called serious 'training'.

5.48 One of the signs of good work is that the footfall of the gaits becomes pure, powerfully energetic, yet uncannily quiet.[8]

5.49 A couple of good, old chestnuts: 'Ride the horse 'uphill'!'; and 'Two-thirds of horse in front of the rider, one-third behind!'

5.50 One of the finest aces up the rider's sleeve is to be non-reactionary to horses' fright, silliness or shying. We need to remain serene, and entirely unaffected – doing so by *concentrating single-mindedly on the work* (gait, school figure, exercise), and not on the horses or their antics, nor especially on that which apparently caused the

---

7 See Müseler, *Riding Logic*.
8 *Dressage Formula*, 3rd Ed., 052, 053, 055, 056.

silliness. It is the rider's task to set the physical and psychological tone of the scene, and through kindness and tactfulness help the horses to become calm and trusting – bringing them under our tea cozy, so to speak.[9]

5.51 With few exceptions, great accomplishments are the result of many small ordinary events done well. A beautiful large tree, for example, results from countless reproductions of the same, ordinary, little cells. If it is healthy, it will bear fruit abundantly and with great ease. The fruit does not make a large tree! A good, healthy, mature tree makes the fruit.

5.52 Clearly, excellence in horsemanship is similarly not built by the 'fruit' (endless exercising of piaffe, passage, flying changes, shoulder-in, half-pass, and extensions). It must be built (that is, it needs to be given time to grow) primarily, though not exclusively, on the pure, correct simplicity of ordinary working gaits, good clear transitions, effective small half-halts, and generally only modest variations in length of stride. Those many small successes help the 'horse tree' to become large and healthy enough to bear some exceptional advanced fruit, which will develop easily and naturally if we do not stray from this central standpoint.

5.53 There is an old Dutch saying that comes to mind, "He who doesn't respect the small isn't worthy of the big".

5.54 It is best to take out the jewels of extreme extension or collection only rarely, saving them for special occasions, and sharing the joy of them discreetly with others; realizing that, when developed correctly, they are the combined precious fruit of having carefully developed our own equestrian talents, and of the gift of the horse's wondrous generosity. There is no surer way to sour willing horses than by over-practicing exercises which require extreme engagement of their powers.

9 *Dressage Formula*, 3rd Ed., 070, 071, 072.

OPPOSITE *Ludwig Koch. Traverse left. Collected trot. Simply perfection.*

5.55 While training, we must take great care to remain ever conscious of preserving the creatures' 'horseness' – it is laughably easy to annihilate. In a misdirected search for gaining accuracy and obedience, we can end up making robots of horses, turning them into a frivolous toy, a caricature of 'tricks on demand' to be frittered away for the sake of entertainment, or just to salve our egos.

5.56 As is commonly known the horses' assessment of the work emanates from their facial expressions. On the positive side, the eye appears serene, trusting, spirited, and attentive, and the ears, radar-like, swivel back and forth as they listen to the rider or test their surroundings. The mouth chews quietly, the tail is gently carried. Furthermore, when the work is good, a fail-safe sign in our physical, 'feeling' department is that the horses are almost without exception easy to sit on, regardless of the degree of collection or extension requested, or the 'bigness' of the natural gaits. This ease is experienced when balance has been well established, and when the horse's back is properly in play, which causes the rider to be carried along with the movement. The seat is completed by the horse.

5.57 When things are inharmonious, the horses are usually difficult to sit on because of the tense back muscles which result in stiff-legged, jarring, cramped, or false, hovering and/or disunited gaits. Psychologically, we may get to see two extremes: on one side of this scale, the horses may be excessively jazzed-up, nervy, frightened, or have a wild, angry or unhappy look in their eyes, the ears may be pinned back, the nostrils pursed, the lips snarling, or the teeth grinding – these signs are often associated with unquietness of the tail. On the other side of the scale, the horses may appear quiet and obedient but we see the listless, resigned or dead expression in their eyes – the creatures' soul, vigour, and desire have departed, similarly disclosing serious offense against their nature.

5.58 Causing any physical damage to a horse with the whip, spurs, or the bit is wholly unacceptable, and utterly indefensible. It is a gross abuse of our stewardship.

A Little Anecdote

5.59 Buddha was once threatened with death by a bandit called Angulimal.

"Then be good enough to fulfill my dying wish", said Buddha. "Cut off the branch of that tree."

One slash of the sword and it was done! "What now?" asked the bandit.

"Put it back again", said Buddha.

The bandit laughed. "You must be crazy to think that anyone can do that."

"On the contrary, it is *you* who are crazy to think that you are mighty because you can wound and destroy. That is the task of children. The mighty know how to create and heal."

(ANTHONY DE MELLO)

Piaffe. Egon von Neindorff on Andalusian stallion Juca. A centaur, demonstrating an exemplary 'connected' seat and position – a seamless part of the horse's energies. Photo by Prof. Ulrich Schnitzer.

CHAPTER VI

Guidelines and Exercises

Dressage is the return of freedom to the horse under rider.
HERMAN KOOPMANS

Introduction

TRAINING, IN THE CLASSICAL TRADITION, is a conditioning of horses to accept and follow our guidance, but doing so as much as humanly possible within the parameters of their nature. Accordingly, our work can only be considered good when it is certified by the horses themselves as being acceptable. To recap briefly, horses demonstrate their approval by:

– the continued calmness, confidence, and eagerness of their mind and spirit;

– the impulsive, balanced purity of the three natural gaits,[1] further reflected by their bodies which grow deep, well-muscled, and beautiful;

– their health, soundness and longevity.

To achieve any measure of equestrian integrity we must hold these simple points as inviolable beacons, the very lodestar for all our interactions with these magnificent creatures.

1 *Dressage Formula*, 3rd Ed., 052, 053, 055, 056.

Towards this end, the hallmark of good training is made evident by the minimal use of physical energy on our part, and most certainly by the absence of hostility. This does not mean that we should not occasionally assert our leadership with a few stronger aids, should that be necessary, but such incidents ought to be exceptional and unequivocally brief. When these occasions have been well handled, the horses will go quietly and kindly on smaller, lighter aids immediately afterwards. If strong aiding becomes the order of the day, and seems to be needed repeatedly or over longer periods, instead of the briefest of seconds, we must seriously question the validity of our philosophy and training system.

Psychologically, if we wish horses to cooperate, we need to help them understand. To help them understand we must be appropriate and consistent in our attitudes, aiding and actions. When they do comprehend, they seldom willfully refuse. If we take these matters to heart and live them faithfully, we will begin to see virtually each horse for the good creature he really is, and how over the months and years of patient training, the habit of responding willingly to our guidance becomes entirely second nature to the horse.

General concepts

6.1 The success of our leadership lies in always listening to the horses as to *how* to lead them.

6.2 Be prepared for the long haul. With short cuts we only shortchange the horses and ourselves.

6.3 First we need to learn, minimally, not to diminish horses by our presence in the saddle, doing so by learning to go with their movements harmoniously. Only then can we actually assist them and improve their way of going through implementing valid gymnastics.

6.4 All of horsemanship exists in any one of its elements: in the half-halt; in forward and down; transitions; the halt; the piaffe; in the working gaits, and so on. Clearly, if we cannot do the simple correctly, we certainly cannot do the complex correctly. However, it is far easier to veil fundamental difficulties under the frills of contrived advanced movements.

6.5 Immediately after 'calm, forward, and straight', the following four points are pivotal in securing consistently good results: **a)** even rhythm; **b)** accurate riding of school figures; **c)** 'keep the neck the same'; **d)** give forward with the hands after each rein aid. An elaboration follows.

6.6 **a)** We need to make a habit of counting rhythm, and help it become uniform and predictable, ticking along with clockwork steadiness. This is found by balancing the horse and by being relaxed and 'resting' in our seat and position, which should continuously participate, dance and flow with the horse's movement.

6.7 **b)** The clarity of purpose in choosing the school figure and its exact size and location is central to our leadership. Besides helping us, as guardians of the riverbanks, to discover where the water (horse's energy, balance) is seeping out, it also quietly and imperceptibly draws the horse to our purposes (**4.21**).[2] School figures can be any of those commonly recommended in most texts or prescribed for competitions, or they can be 'invented'. That which determines a school figure's usefulness, besides the vital aspect of giving the rider purpose, is that it should help in the gymnastic exercising of the horse.

6.8 **c)** It must be our highest priority to *'keep the neck the same'*, i.e. laterally stable, quiet and steady onto the withers and shoulders, especially during, i) *any* guiding aids; and ii) during half-halting or halting, and reining-back (**6.16, 6.25, 6.27**).

6.9 **d)** Of equal importance is the need to have a clear forward-pushing *attitude* with both hands most of the time – especially after every rein aid. Egon von Neindorff's recommendation is to 'push a tea

---

2 *Dressage Formula*, 3rd Ed., 048, 'Introduction: The Practical Use of Exercises'.

trolley'. Others have painted the picture of the reins being like two rods which we push forward. None of these ideas necessarily implies the need to push the hands forward measurably, though one may obviously do so if one wishes to: when lengthening the stride, or when deliberately riding forward and down, for example.³

Bending

6.10 Cradle the shoulders between the reins during bending and changing the rein – be especially aware of the new inside leg, new outside rein when changing the rein.

6.11 **Leg positioning a)** *For work on straight lines, when no bend is wanted in the horse,* both the rider's legs should be in the same position – directly opposite each other, approximately at (directly behind) the girth. This is also the best location for animating the horse. **b)** *For any work when a bend is wanted in the horse* (4.42 'Note'), the rider's inside leg should remain forward at the girth, and the outside leg should be taken back by about a hand's breadth. This is an old, well-established guideline which applies across the board, irrespective of whether single- or two-track work is being asked for. There are some exceptions to this, however. For the first week or so, when introducing leg-yielding or turns on the forehand during the earliest stages of training either horse or rider, it may be necessary to put the yielding leg (the one from which we want the horse to yield) back a little *temporarily,* until the lateral yielding concept is better understood. But, as soon as possible, good lateral responses should be obtained with the rider's yielding leg in its normal 'inside leg' position at the girth. Furthermore, other than for the briefest of corrective measures, once the horse is sufficiently advanced to do shoulder-in, the rider's inside leg must

3 *Dressage Formula,* 3rd Ed., 045, 'Forward and Down'.

OPPOSITE Ludwig Koch. Piaffe. Showing ideal 'uphill' qualities and excellent balance indicated by the vertical weight-bearing front leg.

The author on Barty. Shortened working trot, right. Nicely bent while going deeply through the corner. Here the horse is more 'upright', and is laterally more 'even' under the rider's seat than in the illustrations on p.32. But the poll has gotten too low. More energy is needed to bring the horse better in front of the rider, and therefore also gain the desired raising of the poll.

be at the girth, with the horse beautifully bent around it at the ribcage. If the rider feels the need to put the inside leg back in order to get a (supposed) 'shoulder-in', it is a sign that the horse has not been brought correctly up to the outside aids *in forwardness* from the inside leg, *in single-track work*, and that the horse is not bending properly in his body. Such a 'shoulder-in' could therefore be considered nothing more than a very rudimentary form of leg-yielding (this is often seen in conjunction with the common error of an overbent neck to the inside).[4]

6.12 While bending the horse around the *passive* post of the inside leg, placed at the girth, the standard requirement to 'put the outside leg back by a hand's breadth' not only guards the hindquarters from swinging out, but it gives the horse's ribcage the necessary space to bulge outward during bending. Furthermore, though the inside seat bone should have more forward emphasis during actual bending, it is essential that the outside seat bone *energy* always remains well over the knee on its own side, it must not lag behind (3.13, 3.14).

6.13 With the above concepts in mind, if we do *not* want the ribcage to bulge to the outside (such as horses tend to overdo when going in the direction of their hollow side [i.e., the side of the empty rein]), then the leg on that bulging side needs to be placed a bit more forward near the girth (even if it is the outside leg), while *thinking* of bending the horse around that leg (just hint at it, 'feel' it, do not actually do it). This helps the horse's straightness, and therefore allows the energy to arrive more evenly in both sides of the bridle. As the horse begins to reach more evenly, our legs can then be placed normally once again – inside leg at the girth, outside leg further back, as needed.

6.14 When bending the horse: we should direct the inside heel energy toward the horse's inside front hoof (do not jam it forward), and the outside heel energy toward the horse's outside hind hoof. This is especially significant at the canter.

---

4 See *Dressage Formula* 3rd Ed., 050, 063

6.15 It is a common error to end up bending the neck more, when all we actually want to do is turn the horse.

6.16 The only time in which the neck may be altered laterally is during *deliberate* bending or flexing, when *deliberately* straightening, or when *deliberately* changing the bend from one side to the other. This having been said, the neck is, nevertheless, the least important part of the bending. We need to bend the horse primarily in the body. Just as a matter of interest, the old criterion for the optimum amount of bend in the horse's neck is: we should see no more than a glimpse of the inside eye and nostril rim.

6.17 Are horses actually able to bend in their body, their spine? This is fairly easy to ascertain if we can avoid the blinding effects of preconceived notions, and quietly observe horses when they are lying down (curled up) in their stall, or if we have the opportunity to see them scratching themselves on their flanks or 'where the foal sucks'. That we as riders might have difficulty accessing such spinal flexibility is a different matter altogether. But, just like achieving correct bending (flexing) of the three major joints of the hind legs, bending horses laterally in their spine cannot be forced.

Bending versus guiding

6.18 First, forward energy, assure balance, *then* the guiding/bending aids.

6.19 If horses steer like trucks, they are neither going forward nor are they balanced.

6.20 The motto for all guiding aids, or for half-halting, or rein-back is: 'Both reins even (equal value), keep the neck the same', but see **6.23, 6.25,** and **6.32.**

6.21 We must be able to change the school figure without changing the bend. We must be able to change the bend without changing the school figure. The bending aids may not turn (steer) the horse. The turning (steering) aids may not bend the horse. They are mutually exclusive, and we need to keep their individual function organized clearly, neatly, and separately, in our minds.

6.22 Guiding and bending certainly may be harmoniously combined, but they must not be muddled up.

6.23 Of course it is acceptable to have a bend to the inside, but just because the horse is bent does not mean we have to turn. How else could we ride shoulder-in? Furthermore, just because a horse is *not* bent in the direction we want to go, does not mean we cannot turn if we should wish to. How else could we work a horse on any school figure in counter-bend?

6.24 A well-let-down seat together with suitable position attitudes is indispensable for effective guidance. This mainly revolves around being able to direct the energy from either one or both seat bones exactly as we wish. As an integral part of this, we must be able to turn the upper body from the waist in the direction we are going; and/or be able to turn the hips *with or without* turning the upper body, 'turning the bar stool'.[5] The most common difficulties in guidance lie in: **a)** the inability of the rider to remain evenly let down on both seat bones at all times; **b)** lagging behind in the energy pattern of one or both seat bones; **c)** the upper body is *not* turned in the direction the rider wishes to go (**6.33, b**). These tendencies are more likely to surface when stronger aids are being given.

6.25 Since false, one-sided rein aids are responsible for many common guidance problems, it cannot be sufficiently recommended that we learn to make both reins *absolutely even* **in their influence** (i.e. equal in *value,* as opposed to even in weight or pressure), especially during any guiding (**3.8**). When striving to keep the horse's neck and shoulders stable during half-halting or guiding, we need to keep both hands directly opposite each other, right there above the withers, each remaining strictly on its own side of the neck. Then

---

5 See Wilhelm Mueseler's *Riding Logic:* exercises lying flat on one's back on the floor, lifting one hip off the ground at a time.

think of guiding the whole horse, like one chunk, with emphasis on turning the horse's withers or shoulders (neck reining), instead of the head – doing so without taking the outside rein across the center of the neck. If a horse does not respond readily to the turning influence from the outside rein, a judicious tap of the stick behind the inside leg while confirming the outside rein will help turn the horse (**6.33**). Indispensable to the success of these concepts is to assure that the horse is always reaching steadily into both reins through the appropriate forward influence from our seat/position and legs.

6.26 How can we know when we have achieved equal *influence*, especially when the weight in the reins may at times be uneven due to a horse's one-sidedness? Clearly this can only be tested out and understood while we are riding purposefully. When we are in the process of riding transitions, for example, if we are able to assure that: **a)** the horse's neck remains the same (that is, the bend does *not* change); **b)** the horse remains exactly on the chosen school figure; **c)** the horse remains straight (no lateral evasions of the croup or shoulders), then we have even *influence*. For some solutions on how to help the horse himself to become even in the reins and under the seat see **6.37**.

6.27 Some ways of gaining better understanding of what having 'evenness in the rein *influence*' means, is to experiment with: **a)** bridging the reins; **b)** touching the knuckles together; **c)** placing the hands on the neck; **d)** having the inside of the lower arms gently against our hips; **e)** holding a riding stick across our thumbs; **f)** riding temporarily with both reins in one hand – doing these things until the *feeling* for having this essential, steady, 'two-sided' guidance is better developed, and its benefit on the horse is experienced. Through working with these ideas we discover how the circuit between the two reins becomes complete, literally like a loop; a constant communicative, interactive counterbalancing, one with the other (imagine having a hula hoop in one's hands and through the horse's mouth instead of reins). Through this it will be found that the seat and leg influences will also be more readily 'heard' by the horse. We need to experiment with these good effects and learn to transpose them to the work once the hands are separated again.

6.28 The reason why the horse goes better and is easier to ride with the reins bridged (points **a** to **f**, above) is firstly, because it minimizes the lethal effects of inappropriate one-sided rein action, and secondly, because the circuit is shorted at the hands (the horse's energy comes up one rein to one hand, jumps directly across to the other hand, and goes down the other rein, and back around again.) This takes the arms and the entire upper body out of the equation. The moment we separate the hands, however, the energy circuit between the reins must now be able to travel unrestrictedly through our arms, shoulders, and body as well. This opens a whole can of worms of having to deal with getting correct position attitudes with our arms, shoulders and upper body. Tensions, stiffness, or one-sidedness, *anywhere* in the rider, impede this energy circuit from functioning efficiently, and are the root of many problems (**6.32, 6.33**).

6.29 As we can see, there are two circuits we need to contend with: **a)** the above-described circuit between the reins, and **b)** the circuit of forward energy generated in the horse which must arrive at the bit, travel up the reins, go through the rider, and end up connecting to the horse again via the rider's seat bones (**3.24** to **3.28**).[6]

6.30 A useful exercise to discover the difference between the bending aids and the guiding (steering) aids is as follows (only to be practiced on horses who are at first level or above): **a)** walk on a 10 meter circle with a counter-bend; **b)** walk on the same circle with no bend: a plank-straight horse; **c)** walk on the same circle with the correct bend to the inside. Do each phase for several circles to get the feel for it, and do this on both hands until it is better understood how to guide the horse without changing the bend in the neck. Another useful exercise is to guide the horse at the walk on a straight line (full school, second track, for example) while repeatedly changing the bend, doing so *slowly and deliberately*, however,

---

6 *Dressage Formula*, 3rd Ed., 041.

taking about five or six steps to change from one side to the other, and then staying in any given bend (or in absolute straightness) for about five or six strides before changing back to the other side again, all the while staying exactly on the chosen school figure. The rapid left-right sawing of the neck is to be *strictly* avoided.

6.31 We should think of *driving* horses in the direction we wish them to go, and not *pulling* them there! In conjunction with driving them there, the inside rein may, nevertheless, subtly lead the horses (applies especially to green ones) where we wish them to go (both reins even anyway!). At first, this may appear to be a contradiction; but, no indeed, there is a vast difference between leading and pulling.

6.32 Besides assuring the indispensable presence of correct seat/position attitudes, the main *guiding* aids are the inside seat bone/leg and the outside rein (which must be 'well based' in the outside seat bone/leg by having the outside shoulder nicely back and down [do not turn the upper body outward, however!]). Just *thinking* of the outside rein is enough, because during guiding the reins should act identically with one purpose, like Siamese twins joined at the hip. Tuck the horse nicely into the outside aids with that inside leg (*think* 'circle increase' while passively limiting [receiving] the energy with the outside aids). These are especially important points to heed when riding horses on their stiff sides. When applied in conjunction with feathering the inside rein, most horses will readily become soft and even (**5.31**).

6.33 To guide or turn the horse from the seat only: **a)** be *resting* equally on both sides, inside hip forward ('hips parallel to the horse's hips'); **b)** turn upper body in direction you wish to go ('shoulders parallel to horse's shoulders', but do not exaggerate this, and be sure to keep the outside shoulder well back and down while turning the upper body only *slightly* in); **c)** without changing the seat bones, increase the presence of the inside leg/foot/heel in the stirrup iron (do not jam, just *feel* it gently); **d)** increase the presence of the outside seat and leg and *feel* the whole horse into the direction you wish him to go. This is a subtle guiding influence, forcefulness will not bring success. Remember **6.8**.

6.34 A horse will only consistently follow slight shifts of the rider's weight when the rider remains absolutely central: no leaning, tilting, collapsing.

Straightness

6.35 It is the duty of the rider's outside leg (seat bone) and rein (outside shoulder well back and down) to line up the horse. They align the horse's *outside* shoulder within the stream of energy, so that the horse's head, neck, shoulder, body, and hindquarters become *one piece*, which is essential to achieving independent balance – this counts especially when riding in the direction of the horse's hollow side (**4.41, 4.42** 'Note').

6.36 Normally, the seat bones should have 50-50 equal weight in them (**3.6, 3.9**). When deliberately increasing the emphasis on one seat bone (during bending, changing direction, or cantering on, for example) then we should think of having 55-50. In other words, we should not lighten one seat bone in order to put extra emphasis in the other one. There are many such apparent oxymoronic, counter-intuitive elements in riding which can only be clarified through practical experience. Seat aids are all a good deal more subtle than is generally appreciated.

6.37 What can we do under the following two circumstances: **a)** if a horse is heavier on one rein; **b)** if a horse's back is higher under one seat bone? Usually both phenomena are closely related, and tend to occur and can be resolved simultaneously. Besides the need for serenity and patience, the success of the following recommendations depends on the rider's ability to remain truly central and independently balanced, despite the horse's unevenness and crookedness (review **3.7** to **3.13**). That which is possibly hard to understand (and harder yet to explain!) is that our *influence* needs to remain even, (same concept as **6.25, 6.27**) and yet we need to *passively* accept the horse's unevenness, while using the following simple exercises to assist the horse to become even *between and under* the seat bones. The naturally occurring emphasis (extra pressure) of the seat bone on the horse's high side should *not* be lessened, nor should the lighter weight in the seat bone on the low side be increased, in an attempt to make the *weight* in the seat bones even. That would only cause us to lower ourselves to the horse's crookedness and unevenness (3.31). The solution is to be found *indirectly*, by patiently allowing that steady, *passive*, increased pressure on that one seat bone to remain while we walk the horse on a circle (from volte to 10 meter, no larger) in the direction of that high side. Incidentally, the quieter (the more passive) the reins are during this procedure the more readily the horse will begin to respond to the passive seat attitudes. In due time, the horse will begin to soften on his high side because of that unyielding seat bone pressure, and will then also automatically begin to raise his back better up under the emptier seat bone (which, though lighter, should *always* remain in contact with the saddle, even if the horse has not yet responded to our attempts at resolving the unevenness). This in turn makes it easier to animate the hind leg on the empty side whereby the horse will also begin to take a better contact on the empty rein. Because this procedure encourages equal use of both hind legs, it helps the horse to become even under the seat bones, and to reach evenly into both reins which results in balanced forwardness.

6.38 Seemingly magical pathways open when we discover how to awaken the horse's willing participation. One way to achieve this is to learn how to set up steady, *passive* circumstances or parameters, such as those described in **6.37**, and then let the horse figure out how to make himself comfortable within those circumstances. Horses learn best from lessons which they teach themselves. Other examples of passive exercises are: correct longeing with side reins, and passive bending.[7] All the rider (or longer) needs to do is indicate the school figure and judiciously attend to forwardness.

---

7 *Dressage Formula*, 3rd Ed., 045, p71 point 2, and footnote 14.

6.39 We need to be patient, purposeful and consistent to succeed with exercises like passive bending, or while waiting for horses to settle down when they are excited. While quietly persisting with a suitable school figure and exercise at the walk, it is helpful if we pretend we have all day. Only when horses are calm are they approachable and will they be able to start listening to the aids. To proceed with gymnastic work when the horse is unsettled, other than providing simple guidance, is usually a waste of time (4.32). To run a horse off his feet at the trot thinking to tire him out is also with few exceptions unhelpful.

6.40 The treasure of the horse's willing participation can best be cultivated by remaining fair in our expectations, that is, working within the limits of each horse's level of fitness and training. It is especially crucial to be modest in how much we ask for when things go *well*. If we fail to rest horses *before* fatigue sets in, and continue instead to make more demands, they will be justifiably less prone to offer their energies to us willingly in future. The same holds true if we ask for work which is too advanced, we can expect horses to begin seeking self-protective evasions. As usual, we are the dummies, and the horses suffer. It is a lose-lose situation.

6.41 The good rider is one who consistently strives to let the horse's actual state of development determine the course and rate the training will take. If, in extreme cases, that means needing to hack a youngster or a spoiled horse 'on the buckle' in the countryside for several months, so be it. If, when training a sensitive, 'hot' horse, it means careful building of canter and counter-canter, doing only simple changes of lead for several years before doing flying changes, so be it.

6.42 For the true horseman no work is too menial or rudimentary, and piaffe is not treasured above a *good* working trot. Delight is gained within modesty, based in the rider's respect for horses and a genuine desire to guard and foster their spontaneous willingness above all. Through this we are granted the joy of experiencing the glorious feeling of harmony and playful ease in our riding.

6.43 A useful instrument in the trainer's tool kit is to longe a horse from the saddle (this only means to keep the work very simple, just ticking along on large school figures – as opposed to using a longe line and tack). This applies particularly when working young horses or retraining spoiled ones. The simplicity of such work brings rich rewards but, as with so many things that are uncomplicated, it requires a very experienced rider to do it well. Much of our human thinking tends to be altogether too complex, and when combined with impatience and having difficulty living in the present moment, such concepts usually accrue only indifferent results.

6.44 Success lies not merely in doing recommended exercises, but in how and when we do them. Patterned, cookie-cutter methods become stale and mechanical all too soon. Besides being inflexible to the needs of the living moment, they readily cause horses to anticipate. We need to remain feeling and mentally agile, ever ready to come up with a fresh approach.

6.45 A concept commonly used in jumping can be usefully applied to all riding: 'Throw your heart over the fence and go after it'. Our heart is our desire, our conceptual resolve, of wanting to go 'there' purposefully. This imaginary, ever receding focal point should be well ahead of us (10–15 meters), and we must want to 'go after it' continually. The horses recognize such clarity and usually respond favourably to it. 'Feel what's under you, think of what's out there.'

6.46 Correct 'forward and down' stretching is like a spring blossom which patiently contains the fullness of the autumn harvest.

6.47 When things are right, the rider will always be able to go 'on the buckle', even immediately after sparkling collected work, and have the horse walk on absolutely calmly, stretching his head and neck effortlessly downward, completely unconcerned about the preceding work. Another highly revealing clincher is to be able to ride a good, solid forward and down (nose at, or in front of, the vertical) in any gait, at any moment, at any level of work. These are unfalsifiable proofs of the pudding.

6.48 Let us not wait until things go perfectly before we praise the horse. The qualities of 'recognition' and 'gratitude' are central to fair and viable leadership. Truly, it is essential to realize that horses owe us absolutely nothing, ever! Considering that they almost invariably go well when we ride well, it should be clear that we need to let the rays of our benevolent heart smile on our horses frequently, patting them gently and encouraging them often during the ride, 'Come, let's do this together, you and me ... Good boy!'

A little anecdote

6.49 I once had a student who had a serious case of non-stop fiddleitis with her hands. It was such an ingrained habit that she was entirely oblivious of doing so. Though sincere, conscientious, constructively self-critical and hard-working beyond reproach, she had a devil of a time getting those hands quiet. To help her become more aware, I had to remind her countless upon countless times. I explained, reasoned, encouraged, and in my inimitable way 'hollered' (truly, I do not shout, I *emphasize!*), and encouraged over and over, and prodded yet again ... all seemingly to little or no avail. I finally got so tired of having to do this interminable repetition that something had to be done. Indeed, as the old cliché goes, 'necessity is the mother of invention', and thankfully it was. I got a little bell, and every time those hands moved I would ring that bell. Well, needless to say, it rang an awful lot at first, and my student got more and more frustrated as time went on. This proceeded until she suddenly pulled up short in front of me, and exclaimed, "I can't wait to win the 'no-bell' prize!"

CHAPTER VII

Ever Learning

The realization that he has always yet to learn brings the true rider to dedicate his life to this art.

RICHARD WÄTJEN

Introduction

THIS CHAPTER COVERS WAYS of approaching our riding to help it become more enjoyable and productive – how to benefit more from instruction, as well as some points regarding teaching itself. The subject matter is rounded up with a general guideline for choosing teachers and stables that might be considered better-suited for working in accordance with classical standards.

I ask the reader's forbearance if it appears that the obvious may

OPPOSITE

ABOVE *Margot Huelke on Gitano (¾ Andalusian, ¼ Arab cross, aged 4–5.) Demonstrating an ideal working and training attitude for the young horse. Rider in a fitting, independent, balanced, 'gentle' position for the working trot, rising. Very fine work.*

BELOW *Gitano, collected trot. Approximately 10 years later. A fortuitous comparison shot, capturing the same horse in the identical trot phase as above. Gitano has clearly developed beautifully in muscling and stature due to Margot's excellent, patient work. Here, the author riding during one of his clinics, demonstrating a 'not so perfect' hand position (there is no technical advantage to having such a hand attitude, it is simply incorrect). At this moment the rider has also not as yet resolved independent balance in the horse, which is mirrored in the horse's tension against the left rein. When the rider is right, the horse will always be right. Photo by Alston Wolf.*

occasionally have been stated, but so often it seems that plain things, though lurking right under our noses, are overlooked. They have therefore been included here.

As students

7.1 Good instruction is clearly central to making reasonable progress and avoiding wasting time. But just being present at a lesson, responding robot-like to instructions, or relying on the teacher as a constant source of motivation, is of little value. Here, the old guideline "Seek and ye shall find"[1] surely holds true. Unless we are earnest seekers we can not be helped by either horse or teacher, and we will almost certainly not find. Participating fully in the learning procedure – being wholly there, actively 'thinking with' the moments as they unfold – is essential to progress. In the absence of such exertion, that vital conscious connection between doing certain exercises, giving certain aids, and the reason why they were recommended, cannot be made.

7.2 An essential part of learning is to experiment thoughtfully with the given information, to make it ours by transducing it through our own personal make-up, and building our own wealth of meaningful experience on many different horses.

7.3 We can make the most of our lessons when we learn to take both criticism and accolades entirely impersonally. The more we remain emotionally unaffected by them, seeing them as nothing more than road signs to help us along the way, the more the sluice gates of our being are opened allowing the water of truth to flow through us, enabling us to experience more fully that which we feel from the horse, relative to the choices we have made under the guidance of the teacher.

---

1 Matthew 7:7; Luke 11:9 New King James Version, (Nashville, Tennessee: Thomas Nelson, Inc.) 1982. (Oak Harbor, WA: Logos Research Systems, Inc.) 1994.

7.4 Though some teachers may indeed be more reliable channels of truth than others, wisdom prompts us to follow truth rather than the messenger.

7.5 When mounting up the day after a good ride, it is easy to succumb to the temptation of immediately wanting to get back to those good feelings from the day before. Yet, such attempts often fail because we have allowed ourselves to be seduced by the good moments, which caused us to neglect to take note of the step-by-step details which lead to that success. The remainder of the ride is thus spent in a cloud of frustration, aimlessly seeking those illusive feels. To quote the punch line of a joke, "… looking in a dark room for a black cat, that isn't there!"[2]

7.6 To produce consistently good results tomorrow, we need to become keenly observant and leave memory crumbs along the way today.

7.7 Basic work is often dismissed as being easy, beginnerish stuff. But to think in such terms would be like the construction crew of a great building discarding its foundations just because the roof was finally up. Truly, we love and honour the rose, but seem indifferent towards the stalk, the roots, and even the manure from which the coveted blossom springs. By its very nature, basic work cannot help but fully engage even the most experienced riders among us, requiring constant watchfulness to keep the foundation skills well honed and thoughtfully applied in all work. Tending to these matters has to do with being real, to the core, striving to be in purest harmony with the sacred laws by which horses have their very being. If we could but realize the significance of getting these principle building blocks – the very DNA of horsemanship – right, the body of our work would develop far more predictably and beautifully than we could possibly imagine, and we would not tire of

---

[2] "Two prelates, a Catholic and a Protestant, were having a theological fencing match, a real donnybrook. After numerous impassioned forays, back and forth, out of sheer frustration the Catholic prelate finally blurted, 'You know what's the matter with you Protestants, you're looking in a dark room for a black cat, and you can't find it!' 'Oh, really!' retorted the Protestant, 'Well, you Catholics are looking in a dark room for a black cat, that isn't there!" [author unknown].

wanting to polish these substructures continually, so that we could reap, again and again, the unspeakable joy of working in harmony with nature through the gateway of the horse.

7.8 When in a group lesson, we can gain the most if we let nothing slip our notice and do as though every word from the instructor is directed at us personally, testing ourselves against each concept and, if it should apply, making the necessary adjustments to our approach.

7.9 It takes many years of steeping in a horse-harmonious, horse-centered environment, under the guidance of a capable teacher, before the creatures' hidden truths reveal themselves to us and before we can reliably begin to discern between good work and that which is deficient or flawed. An essential part of this curriculum is to have correct theory right at our mental fingertips through studying the literary works of past masters.[3] It does not matter that it may still take years to perfect the application of that theory, but at least our practice will be more meaningfully directed. It is also worthwhile to keep a diary, and moreover to distill the notes down to brief points that can be easily memorized or quickly reviewed before mounting.

7.10 As with all things the middle ground is to be sought. Without sufficient theory, practice is limited to the repertoire of a backyard hobby. When theory is overemphasized it gets us too much into the intellectual, left side of our minds which overrides the indispensable intuitive, feeling, right side, and thus suppresses the untroubled, childlike spontaneity so essential to fine horsemanship. Nevertheless, just as a pianist needs to play scales, so we initially need the structure of theory and 'imposed' exercises in order to acquire good habits so that our intuition and talents can then gradually begin to take over once again, whereby the performance acquires the desired natural flair.

---

3 Please refer to the Recommended Reading list at the back of this book.

7.11 Some things have to do with more than just technical know-how, physical dexterity, or an individual's IQ. Training is one of those. It has to do with an intuitive feel for the horse, the measure of which is ineffable and unteachable. The good trainer is to the matter born. It takes a talented, experienced rider to train a horse well. Only then can that horse, under the guidance of a good instructor, teach another person how to ride properly. The living 'master-horse-pupil' connection is vital for efficient learning. The reason is, unless one knows what independent, balanced correctness feels like, and has learned to regenerate it consistently over many years on trained horses, in most cases it is extremely difficult to bring an untrained horse to that correct state. To quote Christian Morgenstern, "Those who do not know about the goal, cannot have the way". Certainly, without the support of good instruction, the concept of 'green horse and green rider' is at best a formula for mediocrity, especially when considering the more refined spheres of classical riding. Those who believe the 'green horse/rider' combination is even remotely viable are simply writing off four hundred years of hard-won experience compiled by the greatest riders ever known … anyone for re-inventing the wheel?

7.12 To draw an analogy with the computer world: a person who can ride a trained horse is like an end user, whereas a person who can train is like a programmer.[4]

7.13 Three steps to increased awareness and self-improvement are: a) through instruction and study, *find out* what we need to do; b) while practicing *think* of what we need to do, and actually *do* it; c) rather than waiting to be reminded by someone else, we must diligently, repeatedly, and ceaselessly, *check up on ourselves* to see whether or not we are actually doing what we think we are doing. To bring our ideas and ideals into being we need to 'live what we know' to the best of our ability, each moment of each day.

7.14 Perfection develops only through a process of trial and error. Fear of making mistakes stifles the essential freedom to experiment in

---

4 Concept by Susan Dummit.

the 'living laboratory of the horse' and to find out how to get things just right. On the other hand, we must obviously avoid deliberate carelessness, such as being disrespectful toward the horse or making the same errors over and over again even after they have been pointed out innumerable times. The Dutch have a humorous play on words about this common human failing, it goes something like this: "Is it 'in-*stinct*' or intelligence? ... A donkey rarely bumps itself on the same rock twice, yet the human being '*stinks-into*' it [falls for it] each time again".

7.15 Chocolates, chocolates, chocolates … MMM-mmmmm … we *do* love our old habits …

7.16 Does practice make perfect? Not really. Only good, thoughtful, diligent practice in time brings us closer to perfection. Long hours of incorrect practice can only make us experts at doing things incorrectly. This leads us to a quote on the definition of insanity, "Doing the same thing over and over again, and expecting different results!"[5]

7.17 Needless to say, at times we all make errors in our approach, or do not have a good connection with our body, or are possibly emotionally burdened, and thus find ourselves out of harmony with the horse. But, if we meet such happenings as challenges to be overcome through intelligent assessment and continual effort at self-improvement, we can turn all negatives into positives – problems become pathways to learning and healing. We strive for perfection while acknowledging our imperfection, without being dragged down by it.

7.18 On the other hand, we sound the death knell to any productive work the moment we look away from the simple reality of our task – 'What can I do, here and now, on this day, to **help** this horse, with these symptoms, to go better?' – and begin instead to search for excuses for why the horse is not going well.

---

5 Author unknown (if anyone knows who coined this saying, please notify me, so that a proper acknowledgment can be made).

7.19 It is all really quite simple. If the horse goes poorly, it is the rider's fault. If the horse goes well, it is the rider's 'fault'.

7.20 Riding is replete with 'chicken and egg' situations. The rider is the chicken and the egg.

7.21 Regardless of the degree of our youthful talents, there is no substitute for equestrian maturity.

7.22 The most valuable ribbon, medal, or equestrian certificate is the one awarded by the horse. It can either be presented or rescinded at any moment while the rider occupies the saddle.

7.23 In the 'inner game of riding' the art lies in remaining modest, especially as our talents start to blossom.

7.24 The following points, I believe, are surely worthy of consideration as we set our personal equestrian ideals: **a)** striving ever to improve ourselves to become our own best; **b)** studying to gain an ever deeper understanding of horses, so as to live in ever greater harmony with them; **c)** serving horses by taking the best possible care of them while they are in our stewardship; **d)** being fair and reasonable in our requests of the horse while riding; **e)** being ever grateful for having the privilege of being in the horse's presence.

As teachers

7.25 Besides aspiring to the above ideals on a personal level, the following are high on my list of priorities when I think of establishing teaching ideals: **a)** to foster respect for horses, to be an ambassador for them, a loyal guardian of their needs; **b)** to be respectful of the pupil, to champion sound values and inspire excellence; **c)** to be a mediator between horse and rider, so that harmony can ensue through mutual understanding; **d)** to make oneself obsolete as soon as possible by advocating independence, encouraging students to cultivate the ability to learn directly from the horse, while developing trust in their own abilities; e) to have as one's sole motivation for all guidance, the fulfilling of the specific needs of the horse or rider at any given moment.

7.26 Surely, our riding, training and teaching become impoverished if we let our ambitions, or the superficiality of some arbitrary schedule of external events, such as an impending competition or the age of a horse, rule the rate of training.

7.27 Good example is by far the most incisive message.

7.28 How can we as teachers possibly propagate the highest degree of equestrian truth, unless we are prepared to acknowledge the deficiencies in our own riding, rather than trying to hide or justify them? It is equally important for the student to accept, possibly even appreciate, that every teacher has strengths and weaknesses, and to recognize that both aspects can be instructive simply by striving to emulate the good while avoiding the teacher's personal challenges.

7.29 How much has the rider understood? What are they feeling, thinking, experiencing? Encouraging dialogue enriches the learning/teaching environment; it took a considerable time for me to appreciate that my two-legged pupils needed the same forbearance and encouragement as the four-legged ones who only ever need our patient help, not censure.

By what signs can we recognize suitable teachers, or stables?

The following is not intended to be a black-and-white, 'this is perfection, dismiss the rest' kind of discourse. At the very same time, and despite acknowledging the fact that we all obviously have our human and equestrian weaknesses, it would neither be wise to put discernment aside by turning a blind eye to unacceptable standards of behavior, nor – since examples of 'living perfection' are rare indeed – would it be beneficial to be overly critical. The following is therefore meant as a general directive towards at least the better element of instruction or stabling that may be available.

It is both enriching and wonderful that there are many different teachers, approaches, and riding disciplines to choose from. Accordingly, besides deciding on the type of riding and the tenor of the surroundings to which one's heart may be inclined, each individual needs to find a trainer or instructor with whom they feel comfortable. This having been said, the most essential part of making one's choice is to keep foremost in mind that riding has to do with the nature of the horse, and striving to grow ever more harmonious with it. Therefore, only those teachers and facilities who clearly put the horses first, and treat them kindly and respectfully, should be considered at all seriously as prospects for one's equestrian education.

7.30 **The teachers** "You will know them by their fruits".[6] Indeed, we must not be misled by the sweet words of correct theory alone – anyone can memorize a few key phrases and wax eloquent. As Monty Smith once said to me, "They speak so articulately they could bring tears to a rock, but when you see them ride they bring tears to your eyes". Nevertheless, unless there is obviously either very good work or blatantly unacceptable work going on, it is not possible, especially for a more novice observer, to get a true feeling for an individual's ability by observing just one or two lessons or training sessions. In this regard, auditing fees are indeed a wise investment. They allow us to observe a prospective instructor train and teach over a longer period of time, and thus we can acquire a more fair, well-rounded impression of that person's competence and way of working. While auditing, we need to open our eyes, and make sensitive our hearts, toward the horses and pupils under that person's tutelage.

7.31 **The horses** (Here we must take care not to be baffled by a flourish of advanced movements, but try to pay attention to some revealing

---

6 Matthew 7:16 New King James Version, (Nashville, Tennessee: Thomas Nelson, Inc.) 1982. (Oak Harbor, WA: Logos Research Systems, Inc.) 1994.

details instead.) Are the horses clearly contented; are their eyes full of life, eager and interested; do they go quietly and kindly for the rider; are the gaits elastic, smooth, and pure? Those would be good signs. However, if the horse's eyes are lifeless, fearful, or angry; if the horse seems indifferent, merely mechanically obedient; if the ears are often pinned back; if the tail is constantly swishing; if there is much grinding of teeth; if the gaits appear jarring, and the rider's seat unquiet; or if the horses supposedly go well only after repeated argument, then something is likely amiss, and we should possibly look elsewhere.

7.32 **The students** Do they appear to sit quietly and well; is there an air of serenity in their work; are their aids mostly small and thoughtfully applied; are the horses they ride contented? Those would be acceptable signs. If, however, there is a feeling of unquietness in the school, if riders are yanking their horses about, often using rough aids, or excessive stick and spurs, we can know that good horsemanship is likely not to be found at such an establishment.

7.33 **The stables** Are the horses at peace in their stalls? Do most of them come eagerly to the front of the stall when people approach? Is the general ambience of the barn quiet and horse-friendly? Is the water adequate and clean, is the air sweet, are the stalls clean, is the aisleway orderly? Are the horses in good flesh? If the answer to these questions is affirmative, then the stable is possibly acceptable. If the answer is no, however, one would do well to look further... especially if the horses stay in the back of the stalls when people approach, or if they have sour, or dead, or unhappy expressions on their faces.

Happy, contented horses, and clean, orderly, peaceful surroundings are an indispensable backdrop for positive learning experiences for those who wish to excel in true horsemanship.

OPPOSITE *Ludwig Koch. Canter pirouette left.*

CHAPTER VIII

On Nature

*E*INSTEIN OBSERVED, "Nature does not hide her secrets by way of ruse, but because she is so essentially lofty". Indeed, is it not exactly because the underpinnings from which manifest nature springs are so deeply secreted from our perceptions that, in some indefinable place of our being, a gnawing desire seems ever to linger – unslakable, tenacious – to gain a more significant toehold to understanding. And yet, ironically, as we become ripe to receive and understand them, little by little, the mysteries reveal themselves with apparent nonchalance, reposing as they do with quiet certainty in the awesome power of their truth.

Though we may at times feel remote from finding entirely satisfying solutions, nevertheless, I feel we are given some unexpectedly generous hints, right there in our daily comings and goings, which provide an opportune glimpse into nature's secrets – if, for example, we observe the difference between a stick lying on the forest floor and a living branch. Though both have the same substance, one is a viable manifestation, the other a broken, discarded vessel, to be recycled through nature's clearing house.

Taking this as the basic premise, I sense the Causative Power of this universe plant, represented in the living branch, as being entirely volatile, the very epitome of flexibility which follows principle rather than stagnant structure, and that it pursues one single calling – to manifest *Life* –

OPPOSITE PAGE *That which is Divine is, simply ... divine.*
Image credit: The Hubble Heritage Team (STScI/AURA) and NASA. For details see p.xi

and in doing so honours its Creator: the Life, the Light, the Love, and the Law of the universe.

An insightful adage states, 'Success is a prepared force meeting an opportunity'. That is surely the ultimate interpretation of nature's domain: an entirely fluid, malleable realm, a plasma of charged potential – walled-up Life Force straining at the leash to burst onto the scene, adapting endlessly, mutating uninhibitedly in order to do so. It is constantly interdependent, interactive, symbiotic, irrepressible – plants growing up through concrete – the living, breathing, dancing desire of creation, manifesting physically through an eternal stream of cycling.

Truly, all things physical could be seen as a slow river, always appearing the same, yet only able to manifest through the constant process of replenishment of its elements, just as any one life is constantly being re-represented by new cells which ceaselessly replace the old. The only thing that is unchanging is the 'living will' within, which draws to itself the matter needed in order to manifest tangibly through that cycling. Some embodiments cycle with astonishing speed; others take immense eons to complete the sure-footed Word of their intended destiny ... breathing in ... breathing out ... breathing in ... breathing out ...

The river of horsemanship is surely no exception. In fact, it is here that we can see that thoughts and actions themselves are no less tangible than the bodies of creatures or matter itself. Because how could horsemanship possibly be viably maintained in beauty and health unless its participants earnestly and passionately *desire* to provide it with a continual replenishment of 'horse-harmonious *cells* of action' in their daily riding and handling? And on a larger scale, is it not perpetuated through the steady flow of new horses and dedicated, modest, unpretentious riders over the years?

In light of this, it is clear that the greater our desire and ability to be suitably adaptive – 'volatile' yet lawful – the greater the chances will be of us finding harmony with the ever fluid motion of life as it is written in the horse. So through developing good habits we spontaneously and unconsciously begin to nourish, to honourable advantage, the seed of the moment about to come – punctuated with countless little cycles of aiding to adjust the horse, or of corrections to ourselves towards our intended purpose – whereby the performance begins to take on the appearance of seamless beauty.

Our interaction with the horse is validated when the creature is enhanced, is made more vibrant, more joyful, more glorious, more free, more expressive, more ebullient. But the joy of harmony entirely eludes us the moment we try to forge external symptoms by artifice; or should we perchance stumble upon harmony, to then try to hold the lovely moment still, to keep it to ourselves – plucking it off the conveyer belt of life, so to speak – for then we also come away empty handed. For horsemanship can only manifest through us by us hurling ourselves into it as tenable, dynamic members of its living truth. Otherwise we become no more than an impediment – a dead stick. Let us then strive to work in harmony with natural law – stamped as it is upon our very soul, with conscience as its utterance – and so keep ourselves ever as a living branch on the Living Tree: that all-encompassing Power and Glory and Truth manifesting with infinite variety in that which we call 'Nature'.

Blacksmith Herr Glaser at the forge. Reitinstitut von Neindorff. Each single hour in the saddle is supported by countless hours of groundwork involving a great variety of disciplines, each a highly specialized universe in itself. Photo by Dieter Schuchmann.

Thoughts for 'On the Way'

*I*T IS SURELY THE PROVINCE of but an elite few, superbly talented individuals to free-climb sheer rock faces, in the equestrian sense. Most riders need to take somewhat surer, more well-demarcated paths to the summit, appreciating that the journey to fine horsemanship is a process, a gradual development of individuality, moral character and physical skill, not to mention gaining the broadest possible comprehension and mastery of equestrian principles based on the inexhaustible wisdom of nature. If we seem not to have the patience or the desire to deal with the process, we have surely somewhat misjudged the size of the task that Classical riding sets before us.

In order to approach our ideal with any degree of surety, we need to remain ever close to the serene depths of our heart to hear the subtle, yet laser-like guidance from the inner circle where truth abides. For unless we do, we can so readily become disconnected from this wellhead of vital nourishment by the loudness of the day crowding in against our soul, robbing it of its vitality and sacred purpose. Only through the integrity of untroubled patience can we settle down to accept the process which leads to excellence, instead of being constantly vexed by the journey, like small children in a car who keep wailing, 'Are we there yet?'

In the absence of such understanding, we inevitably fall into the trap of taking shortcuts, which beckon enticingly away from the main road, but seldom lead to harmonious interaction with the horse. We can become so mesmerized by our ambition to attain some arbitrary level of achievement that, in our glazed, myopic stare, we dismiss the living truth only to embrace emptiness – an equestrian moth, spellbound by the dancing flame of unmerited acquisition.

Let us then resolve to devote ourselves to a higher calling, and make it our most passionate quest to climb the true equestrian mountain; that we may, through our travail in the saddle, become a living torch to the ideal, and bring the singular beauty of indissoluble communion with the horse into manifestation, each day again, as well as we possibly can, so that those with seeing eyes and feeling hearts may be inspired to greater purposefulness and joy in their own riding, and in their lives.

Recommended Reading

Riding Logic, Wilhelm Müseler. Published in German, *Reitlehre*, by Paul Parey Verlag. First published in English in 1937 by Methuen & Co. Ltd., London.

Horsemanship, Waldimar Seunig. Originally published in German in 1941, *Von der Koppel bis zur Kapriole*, by Wolfgang Krueger Verlag, reissued by Olms Verlag, Hildesheim, Germany. The English version first appeared in 1956, published by Doubleday & Company, Inc., New York; and by Robert Hale 1958; and by J. A. Allen (in the *Allens Classic Series*) in 2003.

Dressage Riding, Richard L. Wätjen. 6th Edition, in German, published in 1966 by Paul Parey Verlag, Berlin and Hamburg. English edition published by J. A. Allen & Co. Ltd., London 1958.

The Way to Perfect Horsemanship, Üdo Bürger. First published in German as *Vollendete Reitkunst*, by Paul Parey Verlag, Berlin and Hamburg, in 1959. The English edition was published by J. A. Allen & Co. Ltd., London, in 1986, in the *Classics of Horsemanship series*; and in the *Allens Classic Series* 1998.

Reflections on Equestrian Art, Nuno Oliveira. Originally published in France in 1964 by Crépin-Leblonde et cie Editeurs, Paris. The English edition was published by J. A. Allen in 1976.

Historically significant texts

Die Reitkunst im Bilde, Ludwig Koch. Originally published in 1928, Vienna. Reissued in 1976 by George Olms Verlag AG., Hildeshiem, Germany.

Gymnasium des Pferdes, Gustav Steinbrecht. Originally published in German in 1884. The eleventh German edition published by Dr. Rudolf Georgi, Aachen, Germany, in 1980. First published in English, *Gymnasium of the Horse,* in 1995 by Xenophon Press, Cleveland OH, United States. Translation by Helen K. Gibble.

Le Maneige Royal, Antoine de Pluvinel. First published in England, without English translation, in 1969 by J. A. Allen & Co. Ltd., London. The English translated version published by J. A. Allen & Co. Ltd., in 1989. The two J. A. Allen versions were based on an edition published in 1626 by Gottfried Müller in Braunschweig, Germany. English translation by Hilda Nelson.

École de Cavalerie, François Robichon de la Guérinière. Originally published in four parts in France, between 1729 and 1731, culminating in the best-known edition in 1733. Published in England in 1994 by J. A. Allen & Co. Ltd., London. Translated by Jack C. Schuman.

Horsemanship, Xenophon. Published in the German language in 1962, by Erich Hoffmann Verlag, Heidenheim, Germany. The English language edition translated by Professor Morris H. Morgan PhD, published and revised by J. A. Allen in 1962.

CROSS-REFERENCE CONVERSION CHART
for the various *Dressage Formula* editions

3rd Ed.	2nd Ed.	1st Ed.	3rd Ed.	2nd Ed.	1st Ed.	3rd Ed.	2nd Ed.	1st Ed.
001	001	001	035	029	028	069	060A	058
002	002	002	036	030	029	070	060B	—
003	003	003	037	031	030	071	061	—
004	004	004	038	032	031	072	062	—
005	005	005	039	033	032	073	063	059
006	006	006	040	034	033	074	064	060
007	007	007	041	035	034	075	065	061
008	008	008	042	036	035	076	066	062
009	009	009	043	037	036	077	067	063
010	010	010	044	038	037	078	068	064
011	011	011	045	039	038	079	069	065
012	012	012	046	040	039	080	070	066
013	013	013	047	041	040	081	071	067
014	014	014	048	042	—	082	072	068
015	—	—	049	043	042	083	073	069
016	015	015	050	043	—	—	—	—
017	016	016	051	044	043			
018	017	017	052	045	—			
019	—	—	053	045	044			
020	018	018	054	046	045			
021	019	019	055	047	046			
022	021	021	056	048	047			
023	019	019	057	049	047			
024	019	019	058	050	049			
025	020	020	059	051	050			
026	022	022	060	052	051			
027	023	023	061	053	052			
028	025	024	062	054	053			
029	—	—	063	055	054			
030	026	025	064	055	054			
031	027	026	065	056	—			
032	028A	027	066	057	055			
033	028A	—	067	058	056			
034	028B	—	068	059	057			

Index of Illustrations

Author, shoulder-in series on Barty   *page 32*

Author, trot (collected) on Gitano   *page 92*

Author, trot (shortened working) bend right on Barty   *page 80*

Banbury Sampson, trot (extended) at liberty   *page 56*

Blacksmith, Herr Glaser, at the forge   *page 108*

de la Guérinière, François Robichon, piaffe   *page 10*

Gericault, Théodore, *Cheval gris pommelé*, canter pirouette left   *page xvi*

Gericault, Théodore, *Tête du cheval blanc*   *page 54*

Hubble Space Telescope image, galaxy   *page 104*

Huelke, Margot, trot (shortened working) on Pluto   *page 68*

Huelke, Margot, trot (working) on Gitano   *page 92*

Koch, Ludwig, canter (shortened working)   *page 14*

Koch, Ludwig, canter pirouette   *page 102*

Koch, Ludwig, levade   *page 3*

Koch, Ludwig, piaffe   *page 78*

Koch, Ludwig, trot (collected, traverse left)   *page 70*

Koch, Ludwig, walk (collected)   *page 18*

Koch, Ludwig, walk (collected)   *page 31*

Lindenbauer, Ernst, canter   *page 6*

Meixner, Johann, levade   *page 5*

Pluvinel, Antoine de, trot (collected)   *page 64*

Seunig, Waldimar, passage   *page 38*

von Neindorff, Egon, piaffe on Juca   *page 74*

von Neindorff, Egon, traverse right, working trot   *page 20*

Wätjen, Richard, canter (collected)   *page 45*

Wätjen, Richard, canter (working)   *page 45*

Index

activating, animating, driving the horse 4.28, 4.29, 4.30, 5.45
adjustments (instead of corrections) 4.10
aids 4.13
  antonyms 4.2
  attitudes 4.6, 4.7, 5.11
  bending p.79
    body, horse's 6.17
    inside leg, rider's 6.11, 6.12
    neck, horse's 6.15, 6.16
  bending versus guiding p.82
  canter aid, timing 5.40
  categories of aids p.39
  delegating 4.25
  description of 4.1, 4.2
  diagonal 4.42
  driving 4.28, 4.29, 4.30, 5.45
  emotions, rider's 4.10, 4.11
  evenness in reins 4.56, 6.25, 6.27
    even basis of aiding 4.41
    under seat 6.36, 6.37
  exaggeration, training 5.7
  guiding 6.30 – 6.34
  holding 4.33, 4.35, 4.36
  intonation of the aids 4.5
  leadership 4.20, 4.21
  maintaining, shadow aid 4.32
  negative requests 4.9
  praise 6.48
  preventing 4.34, 4.35, 4.36
  principle elements of aiding 4.38
  quantum theory of aiding 4.33
  rein aids 4.55, 4.57
    even influence 6.25 – 6.28
  reins in one hand 4.56, 6.25, 6.27, 6.28
  seat and position, incorrect attitudes 3.36
  sequence of aiding influences 4.26
    sequence for lateral aiding 5.44
  shadow aid 4.32
  singing 4.5
  stick, spur, use of 4.27
  synonyms 4.2
  timing p.66
    driving, and canter 5.40
    half-halt 5.41
      leg-yielding 5.42
      traverse 5.43
  two-sidedness, the basis of aiding 4.41
  unilateral 4.43
  weight aid p.39
ambidexterity 5.15
ambitions 2.8, 7.26
  ideals, personal equestrian 2.8, 7.24
animating, driving the horse 4.28, 4.29, 4.30, 5.45
arms, elbow 3.27
  forearms, hands 3.27, 3.28

B

basic work, power of 7.7
balance 5.46
behind the bit (hand) 5.20, 5.26, 5.27
  behind knee, seat energy 3.14, 4.48
  behind the vertical 5.26, 5.28
    overcoming 5.29
bending p.79
  body 6.17
  neck 6.15, 6.16
billboard 5.25, 5.26
bridle, reaching for 3.14, 3.20, 3.39, 4.50, 5.20, 6.13
  against 5.26
broadening front line 3.20, 3.26, 3.40, 4.26

C

canter aid, timing 5.40
changing the rein 5.15
character 2.7, 2.17, 2.22, p.109
collection 5.52, 5.54, 6.47
competition, judging 2.10, 2.11, 2.12, 7.26

completion of circuit
  body 6.29
  reins 6.28, 6.29
confident riders, attitudes 4.59
correct work, signs of 5.56
  reaching 5.18 – 5.23, 5.27, 5.28
  incorrect work, signs of 5.28, 5.57
create 2.1, 5.59
criteria for correct head position 5.18
cutting in 3.11
cutting out 3.12

D
dancing 2.15, 4.6, 5.16, 6.6
definition of the aids p.39, 4.1, 4.2
delegating 4.25
discipline 5.10
distractions, overcoming 4.7
driving 4.17, 4.23, 4.24, 4.25, 4.28, 5.18, 5.19, 5.34, 6.31
  accepting the 4.28
  hand, driving to justify 3.39
  important factors about activating the horse 4.25, 5.1
  incorrect attitudes of the seat and position 3.36
  influence from the seat 3.20, 3.26, 3.28, 4.26
  nape of neck 3.20, 3.24, 3.25
  non-driving 5.47
  overcome resistance 2.13, 4.50, 5.29
  pushing forward while 4.51
  raising the poll 5.29
  timing of the driving aid 5.40

E
ego 2.7, 3.32, 5.57
elbows and wrists 3.10, 3.20, 3.24, 3.26, 3.27, 3.28, 3.29
  riding horse and hips through 3.39, 3.40, 4.26, 4.41
elegance 3.32, 4.26,
emotions
  horse's 5.2
  general, aiding p.39
  negative 4.59
  rider's 2.6, 4.10, 4.11, 7.3, 7.17
energy over knee 3.14, 3.16, 4.26
equal loading of the horse's legs 6.37
errors, fear of making 7.14, 7.17, 7.18
evenness, achieving 4.41, 5.18, 6.20, 6.25, 6.26, 6.27, 6.36, 6.37
  even rhythm 5.16, 6.5
example, good 7.27
excuses 7.18
exercises to improve the seat 3.16
  difference between half-halting and straightening 4.44
  difference between leg-yielding and driving 4.45
  repetitions, school figures/exercises 5.14, 5.15, 6.44
  warm-up 5.13
experimenting 3.16, 6.27, 7.2, 7.14
extensions 5.52

F
face
  behind vertical 5.26, 5.28
  in front of vertical 5.18, 5.22
fear
  horse's 2.6, 4.24, 5.8, 7.31
  human 4.35, 4.58, 7.14, 7.17, 7.18
feathering 5.31
feedback 3.4
focus, importance of 4.32
footfall 5.48
force 4.49, 6.17, 6.33
  forcing, horse 3.41, 4.50, 4.54, 4.59, 5.2, 5.8, 5.9, 5.31, 6.17, 6.35
  forcing, rider 3.25
forearm 3.27, 3.28
forward and down 5.22, 6.4, 6.9, 6.46, 6.47
forward attitude of position 3.35
framing the horse 4.53
front line 3.23, 3.24, 3.25
  broadening 3.20, 3.26, 3.40, 4.26

G
gaits 4.50, 6.4, 7.31, p.75
  antidotes for nervous or tense horses 5.47
  correct work, signs of 5.48, 5.56
  extension, collection 5.52, 5.54
  footfall 5.48
  leadership 4.21, 4.22
  'on the buckle' 5.12
  shying 5.50
  tense horses 5.47
  working, ordinary 5.13, 5.32
give while driving 4.50

gratitude, recognition 6.48
group lessons, to benefit from 7.8
guidance from the seat and legs 6.33
　firmer 5.11
　one-sided 6.25, 6.27
　passive 4.54
　seat 6.24
　unflappable 4.7
guidance, teacher's 7.3, 7.9, 7.11, 7.25
guiding the horse 3.9, 4.46, p.57,
　6.30 – 6.34

H
habits p.75
　good 2.18, 2.19, 5.14, 6.6, 7.10, 7.16,
　poor 7.15
half-halt p.65, 4.25, 5.32 – 5.38
　difference between half-halting and
　　straightening 4.44
　for guidance 4.46
　timing 5.41
hands 3.38 – 3.43, 4.41, 4.50, 4.51,
　6.5, 6.9
　behind the 5.26, 5.28
　evenness 4.44, 6.27, 6.28
　fiddling 5.23, 6.49
　guiding 6.25, 6.30
　living part of contact 3.39
　lowering 5.29
　pushing forward 4.50, 4.51, 6.5, 6.9
　vertical 3.24
　what may they do? 4.54
harmony, finding 5.16
head, horse's 3.29, 4.41, 4.50, 4.54,
　5.25 – 5.29
　position criteria 5.18
　reaching 6.47
　straightness 6.35
head position, rider's 3.7
Hippocratic oath 5.4
holding 4.33, 4.35, 4.36
horse in front of rider, 5.49

I
ideals, personal equestrian 7.24
　ambitions 2.8
immanent thinking 3.3
incorrect work, signs of 5.28, 5.57
　correct work, signs of 5.48, 5.56, p.57,
　p.75
　reaching 5.18 – 5.23, 5.27, 5.28

in front of rider, horse 3.20, 5.49
in front of vertical, nose 5.22, 6.47
inside leg, outside rein 4.47
inside rein, outside leg 4.48
intentions 2.2, 2.12
intonation of the aids 4.5

J
judging, competition 2.10, 2.11, 2.12

K
knee 3.14, 3.16, 4.26

L
leadership 4.20, 4.21, 6.1
learning
　as students p.94
　as teachers p.99
leg positioning 3.15
leg-yielding and driving, the difference
　4.45
lessons, group, to benefit from 7.8
living part of contact 3.39
living
　horse, our living canvass 2.22
　learning 7.11
　living laboratory of horse 7.14
lungeing
　from the saddle 6.43
　the horse 6.38
　the rider 3.2, 3.16

M
maintaining balance 3.9, 3.13
　elbow 3.28
　posture, suppleness 3.19, 3.31
　rhythm 5.45
　shadow aid 4.32
　seat forward 5.39
mental attitudes, matters of heart and
　mind p.11
　confident riders, attitudes 4.59
　focus 4.32
　mental finger tips, theory 7.9
　negative requests 4.9
　'position', mental, rider's 2.6, 5.8,
　　5.11
　　agility 6.44
　　independence 5.2
　relaxation 4.39
　timid riders, attitudes 4.58

mind, horse's 5.12
mistakes, fear of making 7.14, 7.17, 7.18
modest 2.6, 6.40, 6.42, 7.23, p.106
moral p.109
morality, horse's 4.10

N
nape of neck 3.16, 3.20, 3.24, 3.25, 4.26
nature, about p.105
negative requests 4.9
nose, horse's 5.22

O
obstacles to success 2.6
'on the buckle' 5.12, 5.47, 6.41, 6.47

P
participation 2.14, 6.38, 6.39, 6.40
poll 4.50, 5.18, 5.29
position of horse's head 5.18, 5.25, 5.26
position, rider's physical, (see also seat) 3.17, 3.18
　elbows 3.10, 3.20, 3.24, 3.26, 3.27, 3.28, 3.29
　　riding horse and hips through 3.39, 3.40
　forearms 3.27, 3.28
　front line 3.23, 3.24, 3.25
　knee, sit over 6.12
　leg 3.15, 6.11
　nape of neck 3.25
　ribcage
　　horse's 6.12, 6.13
　　rider's 3.24
　shoulders 3.2, 3.9, 3.10, 3.20, 3.24, 3.25, 4.26, 4.41, 6.28, 6.33, 6.35
　solar plexus 3.24
　wrists 3.10
　'zero' position attitude 3.17, 3.26, 4.26
'position', rider's mental 2.6
praise 4.7, 4.25, 6.48
preventing 4.34, 4.35, 4.36
principle elements of aiding p.22, p.39, 4.38
principles
　classical 5.26, 7.7
　of riding 3.13, 6.5 – 6.9
　training 5.7
　universal 2.7, 2.20, 2.23, p.105
　　'On Nature'
punishment 4.59, 5.10, 5.56, 5.57

R
raising the poll 5.29
reaching 5.18 – 5.23, 5.27, 5.28, 6.47
　evenly 6.13, 6.20
recognition, gratitude 6.48
refresh, rider position 3.19
rein aids 4.55, 4.57
　even reins 5.18, 6.25
　'on the buckle' 6.41, 6.47
　reins in one hand 4.56, 6.25, 6.27, 6.28
relaxation
　mental 4.39
　physical p.22, 3.2, 3.15, 3.16, 3.24, 3.27, 3.28, 6.6
repetitions, school figures/exercises 5.14, 5.15, 6.44
resistance 5.27, 5.30
　feathering 5.31
　overcoming 2.13, 3.20, 4.49, 4.50, 5.29, 5.31
rest, on the triangle 3.6, 3.7, 6.6
rhythm, even 4.50, 5.16, 5.29, 5.31, 5.45, 6.5, 6.6
ribcage
　horse's 6.12, 6.13
　rider's 3.24, 3.25
rising trot 3.16

S
school figures
　leadership 4.21
　repetitions of 5.14, 5.15, 6.44
seat p.23
　arms, elbows and wrists 3.10, 3.20, 3.24, 3.26, 3.27, 3.28, 3.29
　belly flopping 3.36
　driving 3.20, 3.26, 3.28, 3.39, 4.23
　exercises to improve the seat 3.16
　front line p.28, 3.23, 3.24, 3.25
　hands 3.38 – 3.43
　hips, positioning 3.21
　rest on triangle 3.6, 3.7, 3.8
　resistance, overcoming 5.30
　rising trot attitudes 3.16
　seat bones 3.14, 4.26, 6.12, 6.24
　shoulders 3.2, 3.9, 3.10, 3.20, 3.24, 3.25, 4.26, 4.41
　sit squarely 3.9 – 3.13
　triangle 3.6, 3.7
　wrists 3.27
self-improvement, steps to 7.13

sequence
  for lateral aiding 5.44
  of aiding influences 4.26
shadow aid 4.32
short cuts 6.2
shoulder-in 4.46, 5.44, 5.52, 6.23
  leg position for 6.11
shoulders
  horse's 4.42, 4.44, 4.51, 6.8, 6.10,
    6.25, 6.26
  rider's 3.2, 3.9, 3.10, 3.20, 3.24,
    3.25, 4.26, 4.41, 6.28, 6.33, 6.35
shying 5.50
singing 4.5
single-track work 6.11
solar plexus 3.24, 3.25
sour a willing horse 5.54
spur, stick, use of 4.27
stables, teachers, finding suitable p.100,
  7.30 – 7.33
stick, spur, use of 4.27
straightness p.87
  achieving evenness 6.36, 6.37
stretching 3.30
submission 2.14

T
teachers p.99
  deficiencies, justify 7.28
  teachers, stables, finding suitable p.76,
p.100, 7.30 – 7.33
teaching, ideals for 7.25
tensions
  horse's 4.49
  overcoming 5.47, 5.50
  rider's 3.2, 3.16, 3.44, 6.28
theory, significance of 7.9, 7.10, 7.30
  quantum theory of aiding 4.33
think immanently 3.3
timid riders, attitudes 4.58
timing, of aids p.66
  driving 5.40
  half-halt 5.41
  leg-yielding 5.42
  traverse 5.43

'tipping the chair' (Müseler) 3.20, 3.26,
  4.26, 5.47
trainer, characteristics of a 7.11, 7.12,
  7.26, 7.30
training p.57, p.75, 4.3, 4.29, 5.7,
  5.8, 5.47, 5.55, 6.11, 6.40, 6.41, 6.43
  repetitions of exercises or actions
    5.14, 5.15
transitions 3.26, 4.27, 5.18, 5.52, 6.4,
  6.26
triangle, of seat 3.6, 3.8
trot, rising 3.16
trust 5.6
tuning the horse to aids from the seat and
  legs 6.33
turns on the forehand 6.11

U
unilateral aids 4.43
uphill, horse 5.49

V
vertical, rider's body 3.6, 3.7
  behind 3.22, 3.35
vertical, horse's nose in front of 5.18,
  5.22
  behind 5.26, 5.28, 5.29

W
walk 'on the buckle' 5.12
  tensions, overcoming 5.47
warm-up 5.13
weight aid p.39
  equal, two-sidedness 4.41
whip, see stick 4.27
willing participation 2.6, 2.14, 2.15,
  4.27, 4.29, 4.59, 5.11, 5.16, 5.31,
  5.54, 6.38, 6.39, 6.40, 6.42
wrists 3.27

Z
'zero' position 3.17, 3.26, 4.26